Using ICT in Primary English Teaching

D0569312

Using ICT in
Primary English Teaching

Richard Bennett

LearningMatters

First published in 2004 by Learning Matters Ltd.

British Library Cataloguing in Publication Data
A CIP record for this book is available from the British Library.

ISBN 1 903300 42 8

Cover design by Topics – The Creative Partnership
Project management by Deer Park Productions
Typeset by PDQ Typesetting
Printed and bound in Great Britain by Bell & Bain Ltd, Glasgow

Learning Matters Ltd
33 Southernhay East
Exeter EX1 1NX
01392 215560
info@learningmatters.co.uk
www.learningmatters.co.uk

Contents

Introduction

ABOUT THIS BOOK

This book has been written for primary trainee teachers and newly qualified teachers (NQTs), though mentors, subject leaders and Learning Support Assistants (LSAs) will find it a useful resource. It is intended to provide the reader with information, ideas, suggestions and starting points for ICT activities in English and literacy lessons.

For those training as primary teachers there is a requirement to meet standards set out in the DfES Circular *Qualifying to Teach* (QtT) where ICT is identified both as a subject and as a means of support for teaching and learning in other subjects. As English and ICT are recognised as cross-curricular themes in the National Curriculum, many of the activities described in this book are applicable to a range of other subject contexts.

Key features of the book include the following aspects related to the role of ICT in learning and teaching English:

- **an overview of the legislative requirements and framework guidance;**
- **research findings and inspection evidence;**
- **pedagogical and professional guidance;**
- **audit tools to help identify areas of confidence and professional needs;**
- **ideas for classroom activities;**
- **guidance on planning for progression;**
- **suggestions for making effective use of ICT to support teaching;**
- **information on using ICT to aid administration and professional development;**
- **information sources and resources.**

National Curriculum requirements for English and the literacy framework set out in the *Primary National Strategy* are central to the structure and content of this book. It also reflects the conclusions of the Office for Standards in Education (OFSTED) which has recognised the importance of developing children's ICT capabilities within meaningful subject-related contexts. Similarly, the activities described in this book take account of findings that learning is most effective in lessons where the teacher has clearly identified objectives for both English and ICT.

Chapter 1 provides background information on the place of ICT in the teaching of English. It sets out the legislative requirements and national curricular guidance and describes key issues affecting the successful use of ICT. It also provides a useful overview of current research findings and inspection evidence related to English and ICT.

Chapter 2 includes a series of audits in the form of checklists to help you identify areas of strength and aspects in need of development. The first audit covers the ICT skills test for qualified teacher status (QTS); the second examines the ICT skills needed for successful teaching of English; the third addresses skills and knowledge appropriate for supporting planning and administration with ICT.

Chapters 3, 4 and 5 focus on the use of ICT in the classroom by describing a series of ICT activities designed to support pupils' learning in speaking and listening, reading and writing respectively. Progression is indicated for each aspect through the presentation of activities appropriate for the Foundation Stage, Key Stage I, Lower Key Stage 2 and Upper Key Stage 2.

Chapter 6 provides guidance for making use of ICT to support your role as a teacher of English. In addition to suggestions for the production of paper-based resources it looks at ways of making effective use of interactive whiteboards and similar resources for whole-class teaching. It also explores the use of ICT for administration and your professional development.

Chapter 7 explores the management and organisation of resources. There is information here on the management of the curriculum, assessment and record-keeping, time, equipment, space and, of course, people – including children.

Chapter 8 outlines resources appropriate for ICT in supporting the teaching of English in the form of hardware, software and internet-based resources. The hardware section includes information about the use of data projectors, interactive whiteboards, and computer devices such as spellcheckers. The software section covers programs and CD ROMs while the internet section provides information and web links for government and national organisations, websites suitable for primary teachers, websites for children, shareware libraries providing free or low-cost educational programs, and finally information about UK educational software suppliers.

The use of ICT in English teaching has a long and fascinating history in UK primary schools. Some of the earliest educational software was designed to support the teaching of English and word processing has continued to be one of the most common classroom ICT activities. This book aims to provide you with knowledge and confidence to develop your use of ICT in the teaching of English. Skills and techniques can only be improved through hands-on experience – and this is just as applicable to you as a teacher as it is for the children you teach.

Links to all the website references in this book may be found on the Learning Matters website at *www.learningmatters.co.uk/education/usingICT.html*

1 What is ICT and what has it to do with teaching English?

Information and Communication Technology (ICT) as a recognised subject has been in existence in the England since 1998. Over the years it has gone through some revisions and more than a little controversy over its definition but it can be said that there are four views on ICT's role in the classroom.

1   *ICT as a foundation subject* to be studied in its own right, with a distinct knowledge base such as what a computer is, how it works and how it has developed over the years; a set of specific concepts such as data, programming languages, electronic storage media and particular skills such as copying and pasting, saving, printing, dragging and dropping. There are some who argue that children need to be taught the skills and knowledge associated with ICT before they can use them purposefully.

2   *ICT as a learning tool* enabling children to do things better (e.g. enhance the presentation of printed information with a desktop publishing package) or more easily (e.g. finding information using a CD ROM) or to do things they would not otherwise have been able to do (e.g. publish information for a worldwide audience using the internet). There are many who firmly believe that the most effective way to learn ICT skills and knowledge is through using computers and other ICT resources for real, subject-related purposes.

3   *ICT as a teacher*, providing targeted activities matched to the needs of children (e.g. spelling practice, learning how to punctuate a sentence). These focused tasks and activities are usually delivered by a specific computer program. To use these programs, children need to know very little about ICT other than using a mouse and/or typing a few letters or numbers on the keyboard. Consequently, it is argued that this type of activity is of limited value in developing an understanding of the knowledge, skills and concepts associated with ICT.

4   *ICT as a teaching and administrative aid* for teachers, helping them to present information and ideas to children in interesting and attractive ways and easing their workloads by enabling them to record and analyse children's progress, to prepare focused worksheets and to access information and resources they need to enhance their teaching.

As can be seen, all four roles can contribute to the learning and teaching of English. Their value and success is largely dependent upon the needs of the children or teacher, the purpose of the activity for which ICT is being used and the knowledge, skills and confidence of the teacher.

USING ICT TO TEACH ENGLISH

ACTIVITY

What do you consider to be the most significant factors which affect how you use ICT in your teaching of English? Rate each of the following on a four-point scale (0 = no influence, 3 = great influence):

- *your own knowledge of and skills with English;*
- *your understanding of how to teach English;*
- *your personal skills and knowledge of ICT;*
- *your confidence in using ICT;*
- *the quality of the ICT resources available to you;*
- *your knowledge and beliefs about the value of ICT as a tool for learning;*
- *your knowledge of software appropriate for supporting the teaching of English;*
- *your personality and self-perception;*
- *your past experiences as a teacher and as a learner;*
- *the needs of the children;*
- *the personalities and past experiences of the children;*
- *the level of ICT knowledge and skills of the children;*
- *the children's capabilities with English;*
- *the curriculum for English followed by the school;*
- *the curriculum for ICT followed by the school;*
- *the relationship you have with the ICT co-ordinator;*
- *the reliability of the hardware and software available.*

The likelihood is that none of the above will have been scored as zero. Teaching any subject is a complex task which is dependent on a great many factors. It is little wonder that some teachers prefer not to add complications associated with incorporating technology into their work in the classroom. However, there are a great many teachers who make very effective use of ICT to support, enhance or even transform their teaching and children's learning of English. For example, OFSTED schools' inspectors describe the work of one Year 2 class they observed.

CLASSROOM STORY

The pupils had contacted one author directly and she had provided them with resources and posters. E-mail contact with another author had been established via a commercial web site. The class looked at one of the works by an author and were taught how to log on to the web sites of two other authors. The pupils then worked in three ability groups with the teacher and a well-briefed teaching assistant. In the plenary, the pupils talked about the differences, similarities, strengths and weaknesses of e-mail and written mail. The whole class shared the e-mails sent by one group and the written records of another. The pupils' response was excellent. They showed a high level of independence and navigated the technology without teacher assistance.

(OFSTED, 2002c, para. II)

Teachers who make use of ICT in their teaching of English have found that the benefits far outweigh the drawbacks once they have developed the confidence, skills and knowledge needed to plan for effective use of ICT.

FACTORS AFFECTING YOUR USE OF ICT IN TEACHING ENGLISH

In the activity above you indicated a range of different factors which could affect your use of ICT to support the teaching of English. These factors can be sorted into the following categories:

- **Personal issues – personality, confidence, experience, attitudes, beliefs.**
- **Relationship issues – child–teacher, teacher–teacher, parent–teacher.**
- **Child-related issues – their experience, needs, learning styles, behaviour.**
- **Subject-related issues (English) – parts of speech, sentence structure, spelling.**
- **Subject-related issues (ICT) – how computers work, what is the internet.**
- **Curriculum-related issues – school policies, national curricula, schemes of work.**
- **Technology-related issues – making it work, sorting out problems, developing capability.**
- **Pedagogical issues – how to teach, how children learn.**

The significance of these factors will vary from teacher to teacher, from school to school, from lesson to lesson and sometimes from day to day.

In addition, those who are training to become primary teachers in England have to take account of the requirements which must be met to be awarded Qualified Teacher Status (QTS).

PERSONAL ISSUES

Confidence is closely related to experience. If your experiences with ICT have largely been negative, the likelihood is that your confidence will be low. This can lead to a negative cycle: lack of confidence → avoidance → inexperience → lack of confidence. Wishart (1997) suggests that confidence with ICT is closely related to an individual's perceived 'locus of control'. People who feel the computer is in control when they use it have less confidence than those who feel they are in control of the computer. The most effective way of enhancing confidence is through experience. One of the key outcomes of the *Computers for Teachers* scheme (DfES/BECTa, 2001), which provided teachers with low-cost laptop computers, was increased daily use for both administration (from 20% use to 49%) and for teaching (20% to 48%), but also a dramatic increase in an awareness of the computer's potential for learning (30% to 68%). With increased experience and use of ICT comes enhanced confidence and awareness.

RELATIONSHIP ISSUES

The quality of the relationships you develop with colleagues, parents and children are dependent on many factors beyond the scope of this book. However, improving your knowledge and understanding of ways in which ICT can be used to support your teaching of English will undoubtedly enhance your self-esteem and consequently will affect the quality of the relationships you develop. Being well organised and having a clear appreciation of the implications of incorporating ICT into your teaching of English will impinge on the professional relationships you develop with children and hence their parents.

CHILD-RELATED ISSUES

Having an awareness of the way in which children develop knowledge and skills in ICT and English will enable you to target your planning on the needs of the children. This requires knowledge of the curriculum (see below) and an appreciation of the way activities should be planned to ensure children develop ICT capability and English knowledge and skills systematically and progressively. However, a well-planned curriculum which takes no account of the children's anticipated responses or teaching which does not appreciate the way children's minds develop will be unlikely to succeed. Many of the activities described in this book are founded on social constructivist principles which assume that teachers need carefully to scaffold learning experiences for children (see Oldfather et al., 1999). This involves the use of assessment information about children's existing knowledge and skills, an appreciation of the way children learn, an understanding of the subject matter, and careful interventionist teaching which enables children to build on their strengths and confront their misconceptions.

SUBJECT-RELATED ISSUES

While curriculum documentation (see below) provides you with an outline of the content which needs to be covered for the age groups you intend to teach, it is expected that your subject knowledge will be greater than that needed to teach children or meet the requirements for Qualified Teacher Status (QTS). This book focuses on those aspects of ICT and English which are complementary. It should be appreciated that this represents only a subset of the subject matter for both English and ICT. For example, some aspects of English are not appropriate for ICT (e.g. handwriting) and some aspects of ICT are not relevant to English (e.g. using sensors to measure external events).

CURRICULUM-RELATED ISSUES

By law, the curriculum that is taught in English state primary schools must encompass the National Curriculum programmes of study (DfEE/QCA, 1999). In addition, the primary curriculum is heavily influenced by the *Primary National Strategy* (DfES, 2003), a key component of which is the *National Literacy Strategy* (DfEE, 1998). Although the literacy strategy is non-statutory, it sets out a highly detailed framework for the content and structure of literacy lessons, including the daily literacy hour.

The National Curriculum for ICT

Whereas many other countries have had national curricula for many years, the National Curriculum first appeared in English schools in 1989. The 1999 modification of the National Curriculum (DfEE/QCA, 1999) created the subject of Information and Communication Technology (ICT). Until this time there had been some confusion over whether IT was a separate subject, to be taught in isolation, or whether it should be taught through the contexts of other subjects. The 1999 revision attempted to clarify the position by stipulating:

> *Pupils should be given opportunities to apply and develop their ICT capability through the use of ICT tools to support their learning in all subjects (with the exception of physical education at Key Stages 1 and 2).*

> (DfEE/QCA, 1999, p. 39)

The programme of study specifies the main themes or strands for ICT:

- **Finding Things Out.**
- **Developing Ideas and Making Things Happen.**
- **Exchanging and Sharing Information.**
- **Reviewing, Evaluating and Modifying Work as it Progresses.**

Finding Things Out with ICT covers activities such as accessing information on the internet and CD ROM, storing, manipulating and retrieving information with databases, spread-sheets and in other forms such as word-processed documents or computer-based images. Also included under this strand is extracting information from other ICT resources such as video and audio recordings.

The opportunities for developing literacy skills which fall within this theme include:

- **developing skills in searching for information presented with ICT;**
- **evaluating the relevance, accuracy and currency (i.e. is it outdated?) of information and sources;**
- **changing the way information is presented to make it more suitable for a database (e.g. by identifying key words, by summarising and paraphrasing, by sorting information into categories).**

Developing Ideas and Making Things Happen involves the use of ICT equipment to enable children to make decisions and view the consequences of their actions, to model situa-tions, and to give instructions to make ICT equipment behave in particular ways. The English subject-related contexts which are appropriate for this strand include:

- **using a word processor or desktop publishing package (such as MS Publisher) to develop the ideas communicated by text and images;**
- **using and creating branching stories, i.e. those in which the reader can make choices at intervals deciding the course of the story;**
- **creating websites and/or multimedia presentations to communicate information and ideas;**
- **writing instructions in sequence, ultimately to control an ICT device.**

Exchanging and Sharing Information encompasses communication with ICT resources, in the form of text, images, audio and video. Activities within this theme appropriate for English include:

- **producing documents to communicate information using a word processor or desktop publishing package;**
- **combining text and images or multimedia for a specific purpose;**
- **changing the purpose of text, for example to make it suitable for a different audience, to simplify it or to enhance its impact;**
- **sending and receiving e-mails;**
- **planning and creating audio and video recordings.**

Reviewing, Evaluating and Modifying Work as It Progresses embraces all previous aspects of the ICT curriculum. Whenever children are using ICT, they need to reflect on the effectiveness of their work and suggest ways in which it could be improved. This requires and develops an appreciation of the application of ICT to situations in the wider world and an understanding of ways in which ICT tools and resources can be used to solve particular problems and provide anticipated outcomes.

The National Curriculum for English
The National Curriculum programmes of study for English in the primary school include some specific references to ICT:

> Key Stage 1 (ages 5–7) – the range of non-fiction texts pupils should use include ICT-based information texts (En3.7a), pupils should be taught to develop their writing on screen (En3.2b).

> Key Stage 2 (ages 8–11) – recall and re-present important features of a radio or television programme or film (En1.2c), pupils should be given opportunities to listen to recordings (En1.9b), pupils should be taught to draw on information from sound and images to obtain meaning (En2.3d), the texts they read should include ICT-based reference and information materials (En2.9b), pupils should be taught to check their spelling using spellcheckers (En3.4e).

However, the cross-curricular stipulation insists that opportunities for children to develop ICT capability should be planned into all English teaching wherever it is appropriate. Some non-statutory suggestions are made as to how ICT can be used to augment the teaching and learning of English. For example:

> *[Key Stage 2] pupils could use moving images texts (e.g. television, film and multimedia) … to study how words, images and sounds can be combined to convey meaning and emotion'*
>
> (DfEE/QCA, 1999, p. 54)

but the document provides very little specific information or guidance for the inexperienced teacher on how ICT resources should be used to support or enhance children's learning of the English curriculum.

The schemes of work
The Qualifications and Curriculum Authority (QCA) has produced schemes of work for all National Curriculum subjects apart from English and mathematics. The scheme of work for ICT (DfEE/QCA, 1997) sets out a series of 'units' of work for each year group to guide teachers in teaching aspects of the ICT curriculum. In 2003, the scheme of work for ICT was modified to provide more specific examples of activities which could be combined with different subjects (including English and literacy) to provide meaningful contexts for ICT-based tasks (DfES/QCA, 2003). The scheme of work for ICT, together with the update describing the modifications, provide useful information and well-considered examples of activities for developing children's ICT capabilities through a series of focused lessons. The units which the 2003 update identifies as being particularly relevant for English are:

- **Unit ID – Labelling and classifying;**
- **Unit 2A – Writing stories;**
- **Unit 2C – Finding information;**
- **Unit 3A – Combining text and graphics;**
- **Unit 3D – Using e-mail;**
- **Unit 4A – Writing for different audiences;**
- **Unit 6A – Multimedia presentation.**

However, some of the other units could be adapted to provide contexts relevant to the teaching of English.

Many schools follow the QCA scheme of work for ICT but concerns have been expressed that ICT capability is being developed in isolation from subject contexts and hence children are unable to apply their knowledge and skills in ICT:

> Many schools use a systematic approach, often based on the Qualifications and Curriculum Authority scheme of work, to teach ICT skills, knowledge and understanding. However, teachers are much less clear when and when not to use ICT to support other subjects of the curriculum.
>
> (OFSTED, 2002a, para. 8)

Opinions are shifting towards seeing two aspects of ICT (i.e. ICT as a subject and ICT as a tool) as complementary. The head of the British Educational and Communications Technology Agency (BECTa), the body responsible for developing, supporting and advising on the use of ICT in education, and the leader of the Qualifications and Curriculum Authority (QCA), advocate a balanced approach:

> It turns out that schools in which children achieve above national expectations tend to employ a mixed approach. Well-taught, timetabled ICT lessons are combined with regular and purposeful application of ICT across subjects.
>
> (Mills and Walker, 2002, p. 30)

The National Literacy Strategy
The National Literacy Strategy (DfEE, 1998) sets out a clear and highly structured framework for the teaching of literacy through the primary school. Although there is very clear and systematic guidance for teaching every aspect of literacy, the Strategy makes very little mention of the role of ICT. Of the 16 references to ICT, six refer to spell-checkers and the rest focus on aspects of presentation such as bullet-pointing. The Department for Education and Skills has recognised the need for more guidance on the use of ICT literacy lessons and has produced some very useful resources for teachers. Two CD ROM-based professional development packages provide guidance on using ICT to support whole-class teaching (DfES, 2001) and independent work and guided reading (DfES, 2003). In addition, there is a CD ROM containing teaching resources for teaching phonics through whole class teaching (DfES, 2000).

While teachers are finding ways of incorporating ICT into the literacy hour, its structure provides little opportunity for children to engage in sustained work using ICT. Effective use of a word processor to support and enhance children's writing skills, for example, requires uninterrupted periods of work on a computer. Teachers in primary schools with ICT suites are finding ways to make use of ICT to enhance their literacy teaching, however:

CLASSROOM STORY

The teacher used presentational software and a projector to reinforce appropriate sentence composition. A piece of text was shared by all to enable pupils to identify the tenses of verbs and connectives in the sentences. The use of ICT enabled words to be highlighted and underlined to emphasise the teaching points.

The layout of the ICT suite enabled pupils to quickly turn to their computers and practise similar pieces of text to the one used by the teacher. The pupils chose their own style of highlighting and underlining and they proceeded with the task confidently. A lot of learning took place during this part of the lesson with pupils discussing past tenses with one another and the teacher making a note of pupils who were less confident.

The teacher proceeded to lead a shared writing session. The teacher typed in text while pupils offered suggestions and pointed out errors. Some particularly good demonstrations by the teacher showed pupils how to italicise particular words, how to use the spellchecker, and how to select a font and size of lettering. The discussion included the use of different words and punctuation in line with the context in order to improve the writing.

(OFSTED, 2002a, para. 6)

The standards for Qualified Teacher Status
The curriculum for those training to become teachers is constrained by a set of standards (DfES, 2002) which stipulates the competencies which trainee teachers must demonstrate to be awarded Qualified Teacher Status (QTS). The requirements for ICT are very explicit:

Those awarded Qualified Teacher Status must demonstrate ...

2.5   – *They know how to use ICT effectively, both to teach their subject and to support their wider professional role*

3.3.10   – *They use ICT effectively in their teaching*

2.1b   – *They know and understand the curriculum for each of the National Curriculum core subjects, and the frameworks methods and expectations set out in the National Literacy and Numeracy Strategies. They have sufficient understanding of a range of work across the following subjects: ... ICT*

3.3.2b   – *A range of work across the following subjects ... ICT ... independently with advice from an experienced colleague where appropriate.*

The guidance in the handbook which accompanies *Qualifying to Teach* is broadly based to enable it to be applied across all subject contexts and age phases. As a consequence, there are no specific requirements for trainee primary teachers to make use of ICT within their teaching of English. It is therefore left to individual students and tutors to decide the extent to which the ability to make effective use of ICT within their teaching of English needs to be demonstrated.

TECHNOLOGY-RELATED ISSUES

A principal purpose behind providing children with opportunities to make use of ICT resources in the classroom is to develop their ICT capabilities. ICT capability encompasses more than knowing how to turn on a computer, use a keyboard or mouse or fill a printer with paper. Kennewell *et al*. (2000, p. 20) identify five components of ICT capability:

- **Basic skills or routines – e.g. moving the mouse or typing on the keyboard.**
- **Techniques – e.g. copying text from one place to another in a document.**
- **Key concepts – e.g. understanding what is meant by a 'file' or a 'website'.**
- **Processes – multi-stage procedures such as creating a computer-based presentation.**
- **Higher-order skills and knowledge – e.g. recognising when an ICT resource or device might help to solve a problem or assist with a task.**

They suggest that:

- **skills and routines are developed primarily through practice;**
- **techniques are learned either by copying others or through trial and error;**
- **concepts are acquired through verbalisation and by reflection on experience;**
- **processes are developed by combining a series of techniques, initially through the support of an experienced person but ultimately independently;**
- **higher-order skills and knowledge are developed in an environment which encourages exploration and guided investigation.**

These approaches are applicable not only for children but also for you. Think for a moment about the skills, routines, techniques, concepts, processes and higher-order knowledge and skills you would use to search the internet for some text about the Primary National Strategy, copy it into a word processor and change its focus for a different audience. With capability comes confidence and both these attributes are important for successful teaching. Recognising how an ICT process can be scaffolded as a series of skills techniques and concepts is essential for effective teaching.

PEDAGOGICAL ISSUES

Over the years newspaper headlines have reflected views and concerns about the relationship between ICT and literacy:

'Research shows IT boosts literacy' (*Times Educational Supplement*, 14 January 2000)

'Boys spell better by computer' (*Daily Mirror*, 21 December 2000)

'Computers "to replace teachers"' (*Daily Telegraph*, 10 January 2002)

One of the difficulties in trying to make sense of research and inspection evidence is that it is not always made clear how reliable or wide-ranging the findings are. Also, education is a very inexact area of study because it deals with people – what works for one person or group of people in one situation may not be applicable elsewhere.

However, without research or inspection evidence we would have to rely solely on our own experiences or those of immediate colleagues. Research provides us with an opportunity to share in the experiences and ideas of others and use this to help our own understanding.

What follows is an overview of some of the findings of research and inspection reports which indicate some of the potential and the implications for making use of ICT in supporting teaching and learning in literacy. Some of these themes will be developed in the chapters which follow.

RESEARCH SUMMARIES

ICT REDEFINES THE NOTION OF, AND HENCE THE SKILLS ASSOCIATED WITH, 'LITERACY'

Several writers and researchers suggest that the greatest virtue of ICT lies in its ability to present information in a wide variety of forms: text, images, speech, sound clips, animated diagrams, video clips; and in its capacity to permit 'readers' to navigate their own way through the information by the use of hyperlinks.

It is therefore argued that the traditional definition of 'literacy' (i.e. being able to read and write) is inadequate to cover the range of skills now required to access and communicate information. Seymour Papert (1993, p. 10) for example, suggests that traditional literacy should be termed 'letteracy' to indicate its narrower scope.

In 1992 Kevin McGarry wrote a short paper in which he defined over 20 types of literacy ranging from 'cultural literacy' to 'electronic literacy' (McGarry, 1992).

Clearly, children are surrounded by information in a range of forms other than text, and hence teachers need to ensure that they have the skills and knowledge required to be able to use this information efficiently and effectively. As Margaret Meek (1991) observed over ten years ago, 'new literacies develop new illiterates'. It is therefore our responsibility as teachers to ensure that children are properly equipped with the skills and knowledge they need to be able to access, interpret and communicate through all forms of literacy which are relevant to their present and future lives.

ICT CHANGES THE WAY CHILDREN LEARN BY PROVIDING NEW OPPORTUNITIES

Millwood (2000) argues that new and emerging technologies (e.g. digital video, multimedia, online communities) not only provide new opportunities, they change the relationship between the teacher and the learner. Children become creators of information to which the teacher responds. As teachers, we need not only to be aware of the basic skills which have traditionally been associated with literacy but also to be prepared to allow children to gain experience with a wide range of technologies which will enable them to develop new skills and an appreciation of the way information can be communicated in different forms.

ICT ENHANCES LEARNING IN LITERACY

A comprehensive study carried out by Moseley and Higgins (1999) suggests that children whose teachers used ICT to support literacy teaching improve their literacy skills five times more quickly than children whose teachers do not use ICT.

The first ImpacT study (Watson, 1993), which was set up to investigate the effect of ICT on pupils' learning, indicated that the children in schools which made 'high' use of ICT resources tended to perform better in other subjects than children in 'low' use schools. The researchers also noted that ICT enhanced motivation and enjoyment, increased concentration and time spent on tasks, and enabled children to identify their own errors and misunderstandings.

The second ImpaCT study (Harrison *et al.*, 2003) found there was a positive relationship between the quality of a school's ICT resources and the standards of literacy and numeracy of the pupils. In other words, schools with better ICT resources produced children with better results in SATs tests. The study also found that the children achieved better results in a subject if they were in classes where teachers made more effective use of ICT resources to support their teaching of that subject. This was particularly apparent in the teaching and learning of English.

ICT ASSISTS WITH THE DEVELOPMENT OF PUPILS' SPEAKING AND LISTENING SKILLS AND HENCE THEIR ABILITY TO LEARN

A series of studies (e.g. Wegerif and Dawes, 1988; Wegerif and Scrimshaw, 1997; Wegerif, Mercer and Dawes, 1998) has shown that, provided activities are carefully structured, computers can contribute convincingly to the development of children's skills in speaking and listening. Wegerif and Dawes (2002) argue that the ability to communicate through speech is fundamental to all learning and hence time spent on developing pupils' abilities to present their views and to listen to and evaluate the opinions of others is essential to learning. They suggest that classrooms rarely offer opportunities for children to work collaboratively; to discuss, negotiate and to make group decisions – all of which are very important in accessing and manipulating information. By use of carefully structured computer-based activities, children can be helped to make more effective use of 'exploratory talk' to not only develop their speaking and listening skills but to enhance their ability to learn (see Dawes and Wegerif, 1998)

ICT SUPPORTS REAL COLLABORATIVE LEARNING

The literacy hour places considerable emphasis on collaborative learning through shared reading and writing, principally through whole class teaching in which the teacher is in control. McFarlane (1997) highlights ways in which writing can be truly collaborative when a word processor is used, partly because the screen is more public than a piece of paper and also because the ownership of the writing is shared between the 'typist' and the computer. Sheingold *et al.* (1984) suggest it is important for children working together around the computer to have clearly defined roles which they understand (e.g. ' typist' and 'thinkist').

ELECTRONIC BOOKS ASSIST CHILDREN WITH THEIR READING

Lancy and Hayes (1988) showed that reluctant readers spent considerably more time reading interactive books than they did reading printed books. Clearly, the longer a reader spends engaged with text, the more meaning they are likely to extract from it. Medwell (1995, 1998) highlights how talking books improve children's accuracy in reading particularly when also reading the same story with the teacher. Lewin (1996, 2000) points to the value of talking books in enhancing children's comprehension of the text but emphasises that the choice of book is very important. She suggests that 'basic' talking books which sound out only whole words or sentences are more appropriate for beginning readers whereas 'enhanced' books which provide hints for children by sounding out segments of words are more effective for children who are developing independent reading strategies.

WORD PROCESSORS ENABLE CHILDREN TO DEVELOP HIGHER-ORDER SKILLS ASSOCIATED WITH THE COMPOSITION OF WRITING

Hunter (1989) indicates ways in which the word processor enables children to emulate some of the strategies employed by successful writers by helping them focus on the content and structure of their work. Underwood and Underwood (1990) suggest that because word processors enable writers to reshape and reorganise their text it should be renamed an 'ideas organiser'. MacFarlane (1997) stresses the importance of teacher intervention in focusing children's attention on the quality and content of their written work. She argues that the use of a word processor does not automatically enable children to concentrate on higher-order thinking skills. As with 'exploratory talk' (Dawes and Wegerif, 1998), children need to be shown how to make the most effective use of the word processor's capabilities through the provision of carefully structured activities.

WORD PROCESSORS ENABLE CHILDREN TO SPOT THEIR OWN ERRORS AND ENHANCE THE CONTENT OF WHAT THEY WRITE

Bowell et al. (1994) among others have shown that children are more able to identify errors in their printouts than when it is handwritten. It has also been found (e.g. Easingwood, 2000) that children take more pride in their word-processed written work and are therefore more likely to spend time and effort enhancing its content.

ICT CAN PROVIDE SPECIFICALLY TARGETED SUPPORT FOR CHILDREN WITH SPECIAL EDUCATIONAL NEEDS

Talking word processors have been shown to assist those who experience difficulty with word recognition, spelling and reading (e.g. Moseley and Hartas, 1993; Miles, 1994) and talking books enable those with reading difficulties to read stories without being dependent on the teacher (e.g. Taylor, 1996). In addition, hardware devices such as talking computers, touch-sensitive screens and tablets, roller-ball mice, pressure pads, switches and enlarged displays enable those with sensory and motor difficulties to access and interact with computer-based applications and information.

ICT IS MOST EFFECTIVE WHEN IT IS CAREFULLY PLANNED INTO LITERACY LESSONS

OFSTED (2002c) found that the most effective uses of ICT in literacy lessons occur when the teacher has a clear literacy focus and when ICT is chosen to match the objectives for the lesson. Inspectors also found that while teachers were using ICT for independent writing, they were not making full use of ICT resources for shared writing.

TEACHERS OFTEN UNDERESTIMATE WHAT CHILDREN ARE CAPABLE OF DOING

Inspections (e.g. OFSTED, 2001) have noted that teachers often underestimate what children are capable of achieving with ICT and tend to be too accepting of what children produce. Inspectors have also found that there is sometimes a tendency for teachers to 'spoon feed' children, preventing them from developing independence (OFSTED, 2002a). It is suggested that these are indicators of teachers' lack of confidence with ICT and its application to literacy teaching.

THERE IS CONFLICTING EVIDENCE THAT DRILL AND PRACTICE EXERCISES IN BASIC LITERACY SKILLS IMPROVE THE ACCURACY OF PUPILS' WRITTEN WORK

Drill and practice programs provide exercises in specific skills (e.g. spelling, punctuation). For many years there has been controversy over their educational effectiveness (e.g. Papert, 1980; Wood, 1984; Dodds, 1985; Abbot, 2001). Ellis (2001) sets out a convincing body of evidence showing that there is no carry-over from drill and practice programs to pupils' own writing. However, it has been suggested (e.g. Day, 1993) that spelling practice programs which use an approach based on the well-established look–cover–write–check approach (Peters and Cripps, 1990) can be effective, provided the word lists are derived from an analysis of consistent errors in pupils' written work.

Integrated learning systems (ILS) are sophisticated drill and practice programs which select activities for children based on their responses to previous tasks. Research funded by BECTa (1998) found that ILS provided very little enhancement to pupils' basic skills in literacy. By contrast, Underwood (2000) noted that children who used an ILS made at least as good progress as they did with more conventional methods and found, as did BECTa (ibid.), that children's motivation was enhanced through the use of an ILS.

SUMMARY OF KEY POINTS

- **Current practices in the use of ICT to support the teaching and learning of English are influenced by past experiences, legislation and the outcome of schools' inspections and the work of researchers.**

- **Although curriculum documentation describes what children should be taught, it does not provide clear guidance on how ICT should be incorporated with English. However, additional guidance has been provided in the form of CD ROM-based professional development materials.**

- **Many teachers find integrating ICT resources into their teaching an added complication.**

- **A teacher's preferred style of teaching affects the way they make use of ICT – those who prefer didactic, teacher-centred approaches tend to use more drill and practice programs in which the computer is in control of the child, whereas teachers who adopt more child-centred approaches tend to make use of more open-ended activities using content-free software such as word processors.**

- **Drill and practice programs are less effective at supporting children's learning than activities requiring deeper levels of thinking.**

- **ICT has the capacity to change the way in which teachers teach, by raising their awareness of new opportunities (see Loveless et al., 2001).**

- **The most effective approaches are those in which the teacher has a clear appreciation of both the literacy and ICT learning objectives for each lesson and an awareness of the immediate and long-term learning needs of the children.**

2 Auditing your subject knowledge and skills

This chapter focuses on the skills and knowledge which are needed to be able to successfully support teaching and learning in English with ICT. It provides you with a series of self-assessment audits designed to raise your awareness of what you may need to learn to be an effective classroom practitioner.

The checklists which follow cover the following aspects:

- **the skills needed for the QTS Skills Test in ICT;**
- **the ICT skills appropriate for supporting English;**
- **the teaching skills and knowledge required for integrating ICT into English teaching.**

CHECKLIST 1 – AUDITING YOUR SKILLS NEEDED FOR THE QCA SKILLS TEST IN ICT

This audit covers the generic skills which are tested in the ICT Skills Test for Qualified Teacher Status. This book is not intended to prepare you for the Skills Test (see Ferrigan, 2001) but the checklist is included as a reminder of the minimum level of skills you will need to demonstrate to become a teacher.

AUDITING YOUR SKILLS FOR THE ICT QTS SKILLS TEST

Each test covers all six types of office software and will contain a balance of the following kinds of skills. Put a tick beside each skill indicating your level of competence/confidence.

Nil	Weak	OK	Strong	General skills
				Choosing appropriate software to help solve a problem
				Dragging and dropping
				Having more than one application open at a time
				Highlighting
				Making selections by clicking
				Moving information between software (e.g. using the clipboard)
				Navigating around the desktop environment
				Opening items by double clicking with the mouse
				Printing
				Using menus
				How to change the name of files
Nil	**Weak**	**OK**	**Strong**	**Word-processing skills**
				Altering fonts – font, size, style (**bold**, *italic*, <u>underline</u>)
				Text justification – left, right and centre
				Using a spellchecker
				Moving text within a document with 'cut', 'copy' and 'paste'
				Adding or inserting pictures to a document
				Counting the number of words in a document
				Adding a page break to a document
				Altering page orientation – (landscape, portrait)
				Using characters/symbols
				Using find and replace to edit a document
				Using styles to organise a document
				Using styles to alter the presentation of a document efficiently
				Adding page numbers to the footer of a document
				Adding the date to the header of a document
				Changing the margins of a document

Nil	Weak	OK	Strong	E-mail skills
				Recognising an e-mail address
				Sending an e-mail to an individual
				Sending an e-mail to more than one person
				Replying to an e-mail
				Copying an e-mail to another person
				Forwarding an incoming e-mail to another person
				Adding an address to an electronic address book
				Filing incoming and outgoing e-mails
				Adding an attachment to an e-mail
				Receiving and saving an attachment in an e-mail
Nil	Weak	OK	Strong	Database skills
				Searching a database for specific information
				Using Boolean operators (and/or/not) to narrow down searches
				Sorting database records in ascending or descending order
				Adding a record to a database
				Adding fields to a database
				Querying information in a database (e.g. locating all values greater than 10)
				Filtering information in a database (e.g. sorting on all values greater than 10)
				Categorising data into different types (numbers, text, and yes/no (Boolean) types)
Nil	Weak	OK	Strong	Web browser skills
				Recognising a web address (e.g. www or co.uk, etc.)
				Using hyperlinks on websites to connect to other website
				Using the back button
				Using the forward button
				Using the history
				Understanding how to search websites
				Using Boolean operators (and/or/not) to narrow down searches
				Creating bookmarks
				Organising bookmarks into folders
				Downloading files from a website
Nil	Weak	OK	Strong	Spreadsheet skills
				Identifying grid squares in a spreadsheet (e.g. B5)
				Inserting columns into a spreadsheet
				Inserting rows into a spreadsheet
				Sorting spreadsheet or database columns in ascending or descending order
				Converting a spreadsheet into a chart
				Labelling a chart
				Adding simple formulae/functions to cells
				Applying formatting to different types of data including numbers and dates
Nil	Weak	OK	Strong	Presentation skills
				Inserting text and images on a slide
				Inserting a slide in a presentation
				Adding a transition between slides
				Adding buttons to a presentation
				Using timers in a presentation

The ICT Skills Test is designed to assess only one component of the ICT capabilities needed for using ICT successfully in the classroom (i.e. personal ICT skills and competences). To meet the QTS requirements for ICT, trainee teachers must also show they can make effective use of ICT inside and outside the classroom and be able to teach ICT as a subject.

CHECKLIST 2 – AUDITING YOUR SKILLS IN USING ICT TO SUPPORT YOUR TEACHING OF ENGLISH

To make effective use of ICT to support your teaching of English you should try to familiarise yourself with as many of the following skills as possible. This book provides you with ideas as to how you can use these skills to support your teaching and at times explains how to do some of the things which are listed. However, the only way to learn and feel confident in using these skills with children is to practise and make use of as many opportunities as possible to use the skills with children.

AUDITING YOUR SKILLS IN USING ICT TO SUPPORT YOUR TEACHING OF ENGLISH

Put a tick indicating your current level of skill or knowledge in the following areas.

Nil	Weak	OK	Strong	General ICT skills and knowledge
				Saving documents in different formats
				Setting the properties of a document to 'read only' to prevent over-writing
				Digitising your voice
				Using a digital camera and uploading images to a computer
				Using a digital video camera and uploading video clips to a computer
				Explaining what is meant by digital literacy
				Saving documents to different drives including where relevant a network drive
				Loading a CD ROM into a computer
				Knowing how to set up a data projector or plasma screen with a computer
				Knowing how to use an interactive whiteboard
Nil	**Weak**	**OK**	**Strong**	**Word-processing skills**
				Outline the key features of good layout and design of word-processed documents
				Create template documents for completion by children
				Create word banks for use with template documents
				Create drop-down and text fields
				Add words to and edit a spellcheck dictionary
				Tailor text-to-speech functions to suit the needs of different children
				Configure a word processor to suit the needs of different children
				Create a writing frame
				Adapt a base worksheet to meet the needs of children with different English needs
				Adapt a base e-worksheet to meet the needs of children with different ICT needs
				Teach children how to use drag and drop and copy and paste to edit a document
				Use word count, spellchecking and thesaurus with children
				Explain how and when to create an on-screen version of a worksheet
				Use a word processor to create interactive whiteboard activities for use with children
				Insert images in a document from clip art
				Insert images in a document from previously saved files
				Edit the properties of an image in a document (e.g. resize, rotate, flip, text-wrap)
				Set up a folder or bank of pictures and clip art for use with a particular topic
				Explain what is meant by repurposing or re-versioning text
Nil	**Weak**	**OK**	**Strong**	**E-mail skills**
				Recognise an e-mail link on a website
				Know where and how to set up secure e-mail accounts for children
				Know where and how to find safe e-mail partners and projects
				Describe the safeguards which should be taken before allowing children to use e-mail
				Describe the safeguards which should be taken to avoid virus infection by e-mail

Nil	Weak	OK	Strong	Database skills
				Create a simple database for use by children
				Rework an information text so it is suitable for use in a database
				Explain the search features of a database simply
				Use a database to develop children's understanding of information texts

Nil	Weak	OK	Strong	Web browser, CD ROM encyclopaedia and authoring skills
				Explain the difference between browsing and searching for information
				Locate and use child-friendly search engines and directories
				Explain how to narrow down a search
				Explain how to evaluate the reliability of a website (e.g. by checking the URL)
				Create a bookmark list of suitable websites for use by children
				Transfer bookmark lists from one computer to another
				Download text and images and insert into a word document
				Create a simple website with interlinked pages using a word processor or web software
				Create hyperlinks from one document to another

Nil	Weak	OK	Strong	Spreadsheet skills
				Set up a simple spreadsheet to record pupils' progress
				Analyse pupils' results (e.g. by graphing)
				Mail merge data from a spreadsheet to a word processor document

Nil	Weak	OK	Strong	Presentation skills
				Create a presentation to support the teaching of an aspect of English
				Use interactive features (animation and sound effects) to enhance teaching and learning
				Demonstrate how to create a simple presentation
				Add images, sounds and video to a presentation
				Create links from a presentation to internet sites and documents

Nil	Weak	OK	Strong	Graphics skills
				Explain the differences between draw, paint and photo-editing packages
				Create a simple image using a draw package or draw tools
				Create a simple image using a paint package
				Edit an existing image with a photo-editing package
				Add text to an existing image
				Save an image as a JPEG or a GIF to conserve memory

Nil	Weak	OK	Strong	Multimedia authoring skills
				Create a simple multimedia package
				Create links between slides, cards or pages
				Add buttons to a slide
				Add sound or music to an object
				Create simple animations
				Create a simple branching story
				Insert a video clip into a presentation

CHECKLIST 3 – AUDITING YOUR KNOWLEDGE AND SKILLS OF PLANNING AND TEACHING WITH ICT

The third checklist covers your teaching skills and knowledge; your ability to plan, organise and deliver successful English lessons in which ICT is used. Many of the items listed are covered in later chapters of this book. Again, there is no substitute for hands-on experience with children in the classroom and so you need to exploit every opportunity which arises to make use of ICT to support learning and teaching. As will be seen in

Chapter 7, the secret to successful teaching with ICT lies in drawing up a well-organised medium-term plan to ensure that ICT activities taught across the curriculum are cohesive.

AUDITING YOUR KNOWLEDGE AND SKILLS OF PLANNING AND TEACHING WITH ICT

Tick the box which indicates your present level of skill, knowledge or confidence. Use the results to identify your priorities.

Nil	Weak	OK	Strong	General skills and knowledge
				Have a working knowledge of the ICT National Curriculum requirements
				Describe what is meant by 'ICT capability'
				Explain what is meant by an ICT tool
				Recognise the importance of running through an ICT activity before teaching it
				Use the interactive features of an interactive whiteboard to enhance learning
				Explain the difference between drill and practice and problem-solving programs
				Explain the difference between content-free and content-specific software
				List some software appropriate for supporting the teaching of English
				List some websites appropriate for supporting the teaching of English
Nil	**Weak**	**OK**	**Strong**	**Planning skills**
				Recognise opportunities for ICT in subject teaching
				Exploit opportunities for collaborative work around the computer
				Break down an ICT teaching aim into a series of tasks with clear objectives
				Set clear objectives for ICT activities to develop ICT capability
				Draw up an ICT medium-term plan showing how ICT capability is to be developed
				Draw up a medium-term plan for ICT showing how it integrates with other subjects
				Differentiate ICT activities to take account of pupils' levels of ICT capability
				Plan ICT activities which include opportunities to gather assessment evidence
				Assess progress in ICT in relation to objectives
				Record and analyse progress in ICT capability
Nil	**Weak**	**OK**	**Strong**	**Teaching and management skills**
				Know where a computer should be sited and why
				Implement health and safety considerations when using a computer
				Make effective use of other adults to provide informed support for ICT activities
				Recognise when and how to intervene when children are using ICT
				Organise teaching for the integration of a classroom computer
				Organise the children and resources for making effective use of a classroom computer
				Organise teaching to make effective use of time and equipment in a computer suite

SUMMARY OF KEY POINTS

- **The skills covered by the ICT Skills Test form only part of the requirements for QTS.**
- **Well-organised planning is essential for effective use of ICT in subject teaching.**
- **The most effective way to develop the skills and confidence needed is to use them with children in the classroom.**

3 ICT and English in the classroom – speaking and listening

The principal purpose of teaching English is for children to become literate. As we have seen in Chapter 1, being literate in the twenty-first century incorporates more than simply being able to read and write. Children need also to learn how to use, present and make sense of information in a variety of forms, of which text is only one.

The main reason for teaching children with, through and about ICT is to develop their ICT capabilities. Chapter 1 explained how this involves more than developing a set of low-level skills such as learning how to use a mouse; it includes having the capacity to make informed decisions about when and how to make use of technological tools to solve problems and assist with the communication process. Ultimately the aim is for children to employ higher-order thinking skills when making decisions about using ICT resources to assist with problems and tasks.

As we have seen, it is often possible and sometimes desirable to learn about English without the use of ICT. It is also possible to make use of ICT to learn about aspects of English without developing children's ICT capabilities – for example, when children are using a drill and practice program to help improve their spelling. However, with a little thought and some careful planning, ICT activities can be organised which both support learning in English and contribute effectively to the development of children's ICT capabilities.

This chapter not only provides a series of ideas for ICT-based activities to support and enhance the development of children's skills in speaking and listening, it shows how many facets of ICT capability can be developed systematically through meaningful, challenging and interesting English-focused tasks.

ICT can contribute to the development of children's skills of speaking and listening in many ways. For example:

- **through the use of audio recordings such as story tapes;**
- **through digitised speech and multimedia, e.g. talking books;**
- **through the use of videoconferencing;**
- **by providing contexts for collaborative decision-making.**

AUDIO RECORDING

While story tapes offer some opportunities to develop listening skills, the facility for children to record and hear their own and others' voices should not be overlooked. Activities associated with the use of taped audio recording include:

- **listening to story tapes;**
- **using sound effects;**

- interviewing people;
- audio-taping their voices.

USING STORY TAPES

Most schools have story tapes of some sort. These are often used with listening units whereby several sets of headphones can be attached to a single tape recorder. Children are nowadays less familiar with listening to radio programmes than in previous years and many will need to be taught how to listen and how to associate pictures in a book with the words being read. As they progress through the primary school, children can make their own story tapes, initially through the unscripted retelling of familiar stories and ultimately to recording carefully scripted dramatisations with voices and sound effects. Progression in the use of story tapes can be summarised as follows:

LISTENING TO PRE-RECORDED STORY TAPES

Foundation Stage
- Whole class – children taught how to listen and relate story to pictures and words.

Foundation/Key Stage I
- Pairs of children given specific tasks (e.g. closed and extended questions: Who won the race? Why was Rupert unhappy?).

Key Stage I
- More complex tasks to focus attention on elements of the story (e.g. describe the house where Peter lived).

MAKING STORY TAPES

Key Stage I/Lower Key Stage 2
- Retelling familiar stories in their own way;
- telling their own stories on tape;
- listening to their own stories and commenting on their effectiveness.

Lower Key Stage 2
- Recording their own stories, targeting younger listeners;
- evaluating their own and each others' tapes, re-recording if necessary;
- adding sound effects to enhance the story.

Upper Key Stage 2
- Evaluating commercial tapes, agreeing on criteria for evaluation, identifying positive features;
- planning, preparing and recording their own tape;
- using criteria and/or a target audience to evaluate their tape, making improvements to sections of the tape.

SOUND EFFECTS

Sound effects tapes, CDs and files are readily available for virtually any situation. Children of all ages are intrigued by sounds and will speculate on how they are made. As a consequence they can form the basis for a number of activities associated with speaking and listening.

Most PCs are able to play audio CDs as well as CD ROMs, and it is possible to extract audio tracks and edit them. Hence, sound effects can be extracted from sound effects CDs and lengthened, modified or combined to create novel and unique effects and sequences. The internet is another rich source of sound effects. Some search engines (e.g. **www.altavista.com**) have a facility for you to search specifically for sound files.

Progression in the use of sound effects could be arranged as follows:

Identifying sounds – Foundation Stage/Key Stage I
- **Identifying familiar everyday sounds (e.g. animals, household appliances), leading to sequences of sounds (e.g. making tea, shopping, mowing grass);**
- **children discuss and justify their decisions.**

Dramatising sound sequences – Key Stage I/Key Stage 2
- **Groups plan, rehearse and perform drama pieces based on sound sequences produced by the teacher (or other children).**

Editing and sequencing sounds – Key Stage 2
- **Groups sequence sound clips to tell or accompany a story or dramatisation.**

CONDUCTING INTERVIEWS

Since the introduction of portable tape recorders, primary teachers and children have used them effectively to conduct interviews. Clearly, composing appropriate questions to elicit relevant information, responding to answers and evaluating the results of an interview contribute immensely to the development of children's skills of speaking and listening.

In terms of ICT capability, operating a tape recorder requires only very basic skills. However, the ease with which digital audio and video files can be modified using editing software on a computer opens considerable possibilities for applying higher-order skills in the selection, manipulation and processing of information (see *Digitised sound* below).

Progression in conducting interviews using ICT could be arranged as follows.

Interviewing 'experts'

Key Stage I
- **Whole-class activity deciding on questions which need to be asked;**
- **recording the interview;**
- **listening to the tape and extracting the key points from answers.**

Lower Key Stage 2
- **Group-based activity discussing the key issues which need to be addressed;**
- **planning and preparing the questions;**
- **recording the interview;**
- **summarising key points.**

Upper Key Stage 2
- **Whole-class discussion allocating roles, deciding on information required;**
- **small groups – planning and preparing questions;**
- **interviewing;**
- **reviewing and extracting information;**
- **discussing and deciding how to present the information, possibly editing and/or digitising parts of the interview (see below).**

DIGITISED SOUND

Over recent years, increased availability of CD writers, the amount of memory and the speed with which computer systems can process information have meant that even modestly priced computer systems, such as those found in the majority of primary school classrooms, can handle quite lengthy sound files. Most teachers and children are familiar with CD ROM talking books, speaking word processors and spellcheckers. Educational software developers have quickly recognised the value of enabling children to record and add sound clips to their work. These features provide a wealth of opportunities for children to enhance their speaking and listening skills in relation to National Curriculum requirements and the literacy strategy.

Talking books offer more for developing readers than story tapes because some allow the children to interact with the text. In addition to the relevant words being highlighted on screen, some talking stories allow the children to click on individual words to hear them spoken, others include animated sequences linked to specific words helping children associate the text with particular words or sounds. Hence the telling of the story can be under the control of the reader(s).

Progression can be achieved as follows.

Reading talking stories/books:

Foundation Stage
- **Many educational CD ROMs now include spoken instructions linked to on-screen animations. Being able to listen to and follow instructions is a valuable skill.**

Foundation Stage/Lower Key Stage 1
- **Talking stories used in a similar way to story tapes (e.g. connecting a listening unit to the computer so several children can listen using headphones) – the emphasis is on children enjoying stories and learning how books (and talking books) work. As the text is read aloud most talking stories highlight the words being spoken, thereby reinforcing left–right orientation of text and developing phonemic awareness.**

Key Stage 1
- **Using talking stories to reinforce ongoing classwork. For example, listening to a talking version of the current Big Book; carrying out tasks such as: letter recognition; identifying target sounds, words or rhymes within the text; reinforcing the learning of a nursery rhyme or poem; or predicting letter sounds then checking by clicking on the word.**

Lower Key Stage 2
- **Talking books vary in effectiveness for developing listening skills. Some place undue emphasis on animations which bear little relation to the text, and hence are of limited value for enhancing children's abilities to listen and interpret. Learning can be enhanced if children are given specific activities to carry out in conjunction with listening to the text. Some can relate to word- and sentence-level activities (as above) while others could relate to meaning-making either through direct comprehension (e.g. Where did the hare sleep?) or through inference (e.g. Why did the hare go to sleep?).**

Creating talking stories/books:

Many educational word processors and most presentation/multimedia packages include a facility for digitising sounds via a microphone. While this does use a considerable amount of memory, most modern computers are sufficiently well endowed with memory to make the creation of simple talking stories feasible. The technicalities involved are no more complex than using a cassette recorder and are well within the capabilities of Year 2 children.

Key Stage 1/Lower Key Stage 2
- **The outline for a story is drafted by the whole class;**
- **each pair of children is allocated a page to write, illustrate and add their voices. The recording process is very straightforward and hence the children can re-record their voice clips until they are satisfied, to practise and develop their use of voice and expression;**
- **the pages are interlinked by the teacher;**
- **the story is evaluated by the whole class.**

Upper Key Stage 2
- **Group-based evaluation of commercial stories, agreeing on criteria and identifying positive features;**
- **each group plans and prepares their own story, and records appropriate voices;**
- **using criteria and/or a target audience, groups evaluate their stories, making improvements based on feedback.**

Producing a multimedia information package or presentation:

Creating an information source is technically very similar to creating a talking story. However, in terms of content and structure far more decisions need to be made about the way the information is presented and the possible routes which the reader might decide to take. Time needs to be taken to evaluate internet- and CD ROM-based examples before commencing the creation of their own. Decisions need to be made about the needs of the audience and which pieces of information should be presented through text, images, sound clips, video clips or a combination. The key educational advantage of this type of activity is that the children become creators of information rather than receivers.

Upper Key Stage 1/Lower Key Stage 2
For this age group, many of the decisions about content and structure are likely to be made by the teacher. A suggested series of activities could include:

- **evaluating a multimedia source as a whole class; identifying key features about how the information is portrayed and the use of images, text and other resources;**
- **planning the presentation of information using multimedia and allocating content to various groups (e.g. different stages of a trip or individual books written by an author);**
- **each group uses a writing frame or template document to create the content for their 'chunk' of information, adding illustrations from a picture bank or clip-art folder prepared by the teacher;**
- **the pages are interlinked by the teacher;**
- **the package is evaluated by the whole class, with comparisons made between their presentation and the commercial package viewed earlier.**

Upper Key Stage 2
- **As with a talking story, the children need to plan and prepare, making decisions about the content and the means of presentation – e.g. should clips from recorded interviews be included? Should some text be spoken, particularly if the intended audience is very young?**
- **The preparation and creation of the source is similar to that for a talking story except that the children will need to make more decisions about the resources and links which will be included to ensure that the information is conveyed clearly for the reader.**
- **The evaluation of an information source will require objective criteria to take account of the accuracy of the information and the clarity with which the information is portrayed.**

DIGITAL VIDEO

Many digital stills cameras can record up to a minute's worth of digital video. Low-cost digital video (DV) cameras are available for educational use, digital camcorders are now reasonably priced and equipment for digitising normal video recordings is readily obtainable. Video and audio clips can easily be downloaded from the internet and digital sound and video-editing programs abound (e.g. on CDs sold with computer magazines). The technicalities of video filming and editing are now relatively trouble-free enabling children to produce professional-looking films and documentaries very easily, e.g. click on 'Movie creator' at **www.taglearning.com/index.php** and see **www.becta.org.uk/ corporate/display.cfm?section=21&id=2666**

The contribution to aspects of speaking and listening stems not only from working collaboratively on producing interview questions or storyboards and scripts but from delivering words directly to camera, either as an actor or presenter/interviewer.

Progression in digital audio/video editing can be summarised as follows.

Filming digital video and editing 'in camera':

Key Stage I
- **Whole-class storyboarding a 'program' (drama or documentary);**
- **different groups film each scene in sequence: the scene is viewed immediately and re-taken and re-viewed until acceptable;**
- **whole-class activity – simple editing, stitching the different scenes together and deciding on transitions between scenes, sound effects and/or music.**

Lower Key Stage 2
- **Whole class, creating a storyboard;**
- **scenes shot and re-shot without erasing until appropriate – this could be done by groups or as a whole-class event;**
- **'best' clips are edited together using a simple video-editing program – this could be done as a whole-class lesson or by a 'production team'. The filmed sequences could be combined with 'library' clips (downloaded from the internet or extracted from a CD ROM);**
- **whole-class evaluation of the completed video.**

Upper Key Stage 2
- **Whole-class evaluation of a short piece of commercial video (e.g. an advert, a report from a children's news programme, an 'article' from a consumer or travel programme);**
- **discussion identifying the key features of a short documentary film clip;**
- **a short introductory exercise in which the children are given opportunities to use the cameras and editing equipment to learn the basic technicalities;**
- **groups of children produce their own short documentary report by either:**
  - **planning, preparing, shooting and editing;**
  - **or, editing film clips (e.g. from a trip, from commercial source(s) or internet) with linking shots produced by them.**

Note: a short documentary film can be shot and edited in one afternoon once the children have developed the basic skills and have planned and prepared the content for their work.

VIDEOCONFERENCING

Once the province of high-powered business executives, videoconferencing is now within the resource and technical capabilities of most primary schools and their teachers. Webcams are inexpensive and most PCs are provided with conferencing software as standard. All that is required is access to the internet, preferably through a broadband link, a little time and patience to set up the software (following the instructions provided by a step-by-step on-screen wizard), and the web address of another colleague willing to engage in a videoconference. It is advisable to have a clear purpose for the conference.

Contexts for videoconferencing include:

- **providing a platform for presenting work for a remote audience;**
- **discussing an issue which is of relevance to the participants;**
- **finding out about other peoples' daily lives (e.g. to support the study of a contrasting locality);**
- **conducting surveys or interviews to gather information about a specific theme;**
- **consulting an expert or celebrity;**
- **developing aspects of citizenship through, for example, exploring cultural diversity.**

The advantages for children in the use of videoconferencing are that they can gain access to people from different backgrounds without leaving the classroom, providing the children are well prepared for the conference and have a clear understanding of its purpose and their roles.

Contacts can be made informally by teachers or by accessing the information provided on websites such as ePals classroom exchange (**www.epals.com**). For worldwide links, European Schoolnet is suitable for establishing European links (**www.eun.org/eun. org2/eun/en/myeurope/content.cfm?lang=en&ov=6516**) or Ultralab Schools Online (**http://sol.ultralab.anglia.ac.uk/pages/schools_online/schools/**) for UK links.

CONTEXTS FOR COLLABORATIVE DECISION-MAKING

It has been shown that while young children are frequently seated in groups in the primary classroom they are seldom expected or encouraged to work together. Appropriately structured ICT activities can stimulate joint decision-making with the screen as a display which is readily accessible and open to scrutiny by all members of the group.

Many of the activities listed in the previous sections provide opportunities for children to work collaboratively. The following activities are designed specifically to develop aspects of higher-order thinking and decision-making largely through providing contexts for 'exploratory talk'. As we have seen in Chapter 1, the nurturing of exploratory talk requires careful planning and preparation by the teacher to ensure children are clear about their roles and responsibilities.

Branching stories offer excellent opportunities for children to engage in true collaborative discussion, provided they are instructed initially in how to collaborate effectively. There are very few commercial or online branching stories currently available (see **www.chester.ac.uk/education/primary_resources/stories** for examples) but it is possible for teachers to produce their own (see Chapter 6) or for older children to write them for each other or younger schoolmates.

The most productive branching stories are those which are well matched to the needs and interests of the children and provide stimulating situations to engage the children's involvement.

The most effective way to ensure all the children participate in the decision-making process when following a branching story is to agree a set of rules. For example:

- **the page must be read out loud for all to follow;**
- **every child in the group must be asked for their opinion on what to do next;**
- **a reason must be given for that choice of action;**
- **everyone's idea must be discussed;**
- **everyone must agree on the decision before a choice is made.**

(See **www.mape.org.uk/curriculum/english/exploratory.htm** or **www.thinkingtogether.org.uk**) for more information.

Progression in the use of ICT to support higher-order thinking and decision-making can be managed as follows:

Draw activities:

Foundation Stage
- **Simple draw programs such as MyWorld provide opportunities for children to make choices, then see and justify the results of their decision-making.**
- **Ready-made screens, such as Dressing Teddy can be used, or teachers can make their own to relate to specific topics or themes.**
- **Children need to be guided or supervised to ensure they work together and discuss the reasons for their choices.**

Key Stage 1
- **The above can be extended by the use of more complex screens and scenarios (e.g. Make a Town)**

Reading branching stories:

Key Stage 1
- **Children need to be instructed beforehand (e.g. as a whole class) in how to ensure all children's opinions are taken into account before a choice is made.**
- **Simple branching stories based on familiar themes (e.g. fairy tales) used to reinforce story sequencing or to enable children to explore 'what if ...' alternatives.**

Lower Key Stage 2
- **Branching stories are more effective if the situation is familiar to the children and presents them with a moral dilemma. For example, in 'Kate's Choice' (http:// vtc.ngfl.gov.uk/uploads/text/kateweb-7078.dcr), the children must help Kate decide what to do when her friend confides that he has stolen some chocolates for his sick mother. Exploratory talk encourages the children to empathise with the characters and rationalise their decisions for the actions to be taken.**

Creating branching stories:

Lower Key Stage 2

- The story is planned by the whole class using a simple flowchart storyboard (see diagram below) pinned to the wall or on a whiteboard;

- pages are allocated to pairs of children for completion;

- pages are interlinked by the teacher as web pages, or using hyperlinks in a word processor or presentation package, or as action buttons in a multimedia authoring package (see www.chester.ac.uk/education/primary_ resources for examples of each);

- the story is evaluated as a whole-class lesson. At this point some pages might have to be altered to enable the story to be read more easily. This could be done as a group-based activity by the original writers or as a shared writing task by the whole class.

Upper Key Stage 2

Children could be shown through a series of focused tasks how to use one of the packages mentioned above, or use could be made of a dedicated story-making package.

- Groups plan their own branching stories using a flowchart storyboard (as below);

- the pages are allocated within the groups for creation;

- the pages are interlinked by the group;

- the story is evaluated by the group and amendments made to improve the continuity and quality of descriptions or to enhance tension or anticipation;

- the story is shared with the whole class for evaluation.

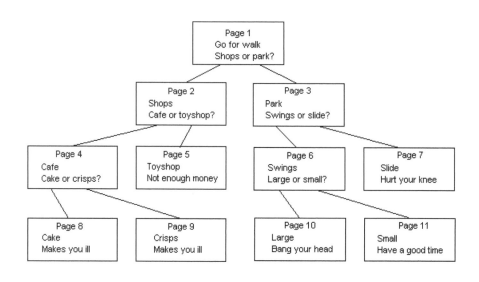

SUMMARY OF KEY POINTS

- Many ICT-based activities used for supporting the development of speaking and listening skills can be differentiated to progressively develop pupils' ICT capabilities.

- Sound effects tapes and CDs can be used effectively to support the development of listening skills.

- Most modern computers include facilities to digitise sounds and voices.

- Creating and editing digital video clips is relatively straightforward and provides ample opportunities for developing speaking and listening skills.

- Computer-based activities are very effective for supporting collaborative decision-making, provided the children have a clear understanding of their roles and the purposes of the task.

4 ICT and English in the classroom – reading

A wealth of CD ROM-based programs exist to provide practice and reinforcement for various aspects of reading. These range from computer-based drill and practice exercises for phonics skills reinforcement and word recognition, through various comprehension tasks to talking books. An overview of the relative merits of different types of reading support software is provided by Bennett and Pearson (2002) which concludes that few programs provide all the support required to develop aspects of reading development and so it is important for the teacher to be selective.

Another important consideration is the close link between reading and writing. It has been suggested (see National Literacy Strategy, 1998, p. 5) that the two develop in tandem; while some features provided by ICT will support the reading process independently, it should be borne in mind that activities which link reading with writing are likely to be more productive.

Also, it has been argued in Chapter 1 that literacy involves more than being able to decipher text. In today's world it is equally important for children and their teachers to be aware of the ways in which information can be conveyed through other media, including pictures, diagrams, sounds, animations and video.

Finally, as has been mentioned previously, while it is possible for drill and practice computer programs to develop discrete aspects of literacy, a key principle underlying this book is to explore ways in which ICT-based activities can be used to develop both literacy skills and ICT capabilities. Hence, valuable computer time and, more importantly, the time and effort required to plan and prepare ICT-based activities are maximised in terms of learning gains.

With this in mind the following activities could be the most productive:

- **constructive use of talking books, branching stories and adventure programs;**
- **word-processing tasks which involve extracting meaning from text;**
- **the use of CD ROM encyclopaedias and the internet for locating, identifying and extracting text-based and other information;**
- **responding to e-mails;**
- **text manipulation and problem-solving programs (e.g. Discloze).**

TALKING BOOKS, BRANCHING STORIES AND ADVENTURE PROGRAMS

TALKING BOOKS

Research studies have shown the value of talking books and word processors, particularly for children with learning difficulties (see Chapter 1). However, as with any teaching resource, talking books need to be integrated into a planned programme of learning activities if they are to prove successful.

Some ideas for the application of talking books to support the development of children's reading include the following.

Foundation Stage
- **At this stage the most effective types of talking book are those which read complete sentences, highlighting words as they are spoken. The children come to associate written words with speech and will begin to recognise key aspects of text (words as units, left to right, punctuation). However, these features will need to be emphasised by the teacher or supervising adult.**

Key Stage 1
- **As children develop some independence in reading, they need to progress to talking books which enable them to interact with the text. Some talking books allow the children to click on individual 'unknown' words to provide cues such as sounding the onset and rime separately. These are much more valuable for a beginning reader.**

Lower Key Stage 2
- **Once the fundamentals of reading have been established talking books take on a different significance. They can still be used to support those needing additional help, but need to be chosen wisely to ensure the subject matter is appropriate. Stylistic issues such as pace, tone and intonation can be stressed, particularly if the children are beginning to work on their own talking books (see Chapter 3).**

BRANCHING STORIES AND ADVENTURE PROGRAMS

The value of branching stories for the development of speaking and listening skills has been highlighted in the previous chapter, however, it should also be noted that to be able to work through a branching story successfully, children need to engage with the text, not only to extract direct meaning but also to infer, from subtextual cues and nuances, insights into the writer's intentions. This will, of course, be largely dependent on the quality of the story and the level of discussion which it provokes.

Adventure programs provide excellent opportunities for children to work closely with text. The simplest form of adventure program is the branching story, where the decisions to be made are clearly defined multiple choices. The most advanced adventure programs require the 'reader' to role-play, guiding a character (or several characters) through complex situations. Educational adventure programs usually lie between the two extremes, providing some structure by guiding choices and introducing problems to be solved, sometimes away from the computer. Their value in terms of reading development comes from the necessity to read and interpret all the information provided (textual, graphical and sometimes speech, sounds and video clips) to anticipate the consequences of their actions, and then to evaluate the outcomes. Some adventures are accessible via the internet as demonstrations (e.g. **www.thebigbus.com/activities/demo/otherdemo.html**); some demonstrations are downloadable from the internet (e.g. **www. topologika.co.uk/demo/stig.exe**) and some can be purchased on CD ROM. The advantages of having CD ROM-based versions are ease and consistency of access and the ability to configure the program to meet the needs of the children and the constraints of time.

The most appropriate adventure programs for supporting reading development in the primary classroom are those which combine text-based information (i.e. telling the story) with some simple graphics to enhance interest and motivation.

Progression in the use of branching stories and adventure programs to support reading development can be achieved as follows.

Key Stage 1
- **Introduce the notion of interactivity through a carefully chosen branching story. Initially, this can be solved as a whole-class activity, later progressing to children working together on stories in small groups (maximum of four per computer).**

Lower Key Stage 2
- **The children progress to more complex branching stories, with situations which require more demanding decision-making, forcing them to read the text and contextual cues and clues very carefully;**
- **simple text adventures are introduced.**

Key Stage 1/Lower Key Stage 2
- **Adventures which combine multiple choice decisions with some problem-solving situations are the most effective for this age group;**
- **the children should be shown how to record their progress through note-making to enable them to retrace their steps if necessary;**
- **more complex adventures can be introduced which require the making of a map to record the children's progress.**

Upper Key Stage 2
- **Adventures which present more open-ended decisions such as whether a character should carry certain equipment or whether it should progress, turn back or follow another route;**
- **the most advanced adventure programs require the children to communicate with other characters in the story to elicit relevant information, seek advice or carry out tasks.**

Software is available via the internet for teachers and children to make their own adventures (e.g. Quest, ADRIFT and Adventure Maker) thus ensuring that the content is relevant to the interests and capabilities of the children. However, writing adventures is very time-consuming.

WORD-PROCESSING TASKS

Word-processing tasks are primarily activities which have been prepared by the teacher, though increasingly these are available on the internet through, for example, the NGfL Teachers' Resource Exchange (**http://tre.ngfl.gov.uk/**). Similarly, some commercial websites such as that provided for TextEase (**www.textease.com**) and Clicker (**www.cricksoft.co.uk**) provide downloadable resources for use with children. Many other organisations provide internet sites which serve a similar purpose, but the difficulty is the time it takes to track down precisely the activity required. Invariably, teachers have to adapt the activity to suit the needs of their children or their teaching style and so it is often quicker for teachers to produce their own.

In the main, word-processing activities are little more than electronic worksheets which children complete on screen. The advantages offered by word processor-based e-worksheets over paper-based versions are:

- **electronic features such as speech and spellchecking can be used;**
- **colourful images, animations and sound or video clips can be incorporated to enhance motivation and to exemplify good presentation;**
- **some interactivity can be included through the use of hyperlinks (e.g. *click here to see the correct answer*);**
- **e-worksheets can be readily adapted by the teacher to meet the specific needs of groups or individuals.**

The disadvantage of e-worksheets over commercially produced drill and practice exercises is that they seldom provide feedback for the children and hence require printing out and marking (though some TextEase worksheets do include automatic feedback for the children).

Most educational word processors include a text-to-speech facility whereby text is read by the computer. Thus instructions, phonemes, onsets, rimes, unknown words or sentences can be read to the children without the need to seek the assistance of an adult.

The types of word-processing activity which teachers can prepare to support reading development include:

- **word-level activities such as dragging and dropping or copying and pasting words into word families, adding rimes to onsets, adding prefixes, constructing compound words, adding connectives, matching pictures to initial sounds, etc.;**
- **sentence-level activities such as cloze, sentence completion, adding punctuation, etc.;**

- **text-level activities including sequencing sentences by cutting and pasting and changing focus or meaning by replacing key words.**

Progression in terms of reading development is largely determined by the needs of the children and the stage they have reached, but progression in ICT capability can be achieved as follows.

Using the editing features of a word processor to support reading development:

Lower Key Stage I
Using a word or picture bank, or dragging and dropping to:

- **sort pictures and words by initial sounds;**
- **match initial sounds to pictures;**
- **sort words into rhyming sets;**
- **add onsets to rimes.**

Upper Key Stage I
Copying/cutting and pasting to:

- **add letter strings to complete words;**
- **sort words into families;**
- **create compound words;**
- **complete cloze passages;**
- **sequence words and sentences.**

Key Stage 2
Using editing tools to:

- **find and replace words or phrases in passages of text. For example, occurrences of 'said' can be found and replaced with alternatives;**
- **alter the mood of a passage by replacing all the adjectives (e.g. happy to sad, peaceful to frightening, slow to fast, lethargic to energetic, etc.);**
- **replace mundane words with more interesting alternatives through the use of a thesaurus;**
- **change the appearance of text to enhance its impact (e.g. through bullet-points, use of headings and subheadings, highlighting key words or phrases, etc.).**

CD ROM ENCYCLOPAEDIAS AND THE INTERNET

The skill of searching for relevant text-based and picture-related information is a key component of reading for meaning. Being able to use indexes, contents lists, search tools and browsing using hyperlinks are essential skills, as are skimming and scanning for key words or locating pictures and reading around them. Electronic texts are no less important than paper-based sources and children need to develop systematic, structured approaches to ensure that information is located, evaluated and accessed efficiently and speedily.

Various activities can be used, not only within the context of English lessons but across most areas of the curriculum to enable children to develop the literacy and ICT skills needed for reading for information:

Foundation Stage
- **Sorting pictures into categories (e.g. size, colour, animate/inanimate, etc.) with object-oriented drawing packages such as MyWorld.**

Key Stage I/Lower Key Stage 2
- **Using e-worksheets created by the teacher to find the answers to specific questions by clicking on links to 'safe' websites checked by the teacher (e.g. History Treasure Trails –** www.mape.org.uk/kids/index.htm**, Internet Worksheets –** www.chester.ac.uk/education/primary_ resources **and Webquests –** www.webquest.org**);**
- **following hyperlinks on web pages or in multimedia encyclopaedias to locate information – recognising the value of this approach when searching for general background information rather than the answer to a specific enquiry.**

Lower Key Stage 2
- **Using 'safe' search engines (e.g.** www.yahooligans.com **or** www.ajkids.com/**) to locate the answers to specific questions. It is important that the searches are purposeful and relate to real enquiries relevant to the children's ongoing class work, rather than separate search exercises;**
- **narrowing down or broadening their searches by steadily increasing the number of key words in a search or by using the advanced search tools provided by most search engines or CD ROM encyclopaedias;**
- **skimming and scanning web pages provided by 'hits' to ascertain their relevance and deciding when their search terms are or are not providing them with the sorts of information they need. Using the 'Find (on this page)' option to search a page for a key word;**
- **'reading' animated diagrams and cross-sections in CD ROM packages. Note: animated diagrams sometimes bridge the conceptual gap that children have in recognising the relationship between stylised diagrams and what they represent;**
- **producing their own diagrams and maps using specific software and draw files such as 'Make a town' from MyWorld.**

Upper Key Stage 2
- **Deciding when the internet or CD encyclopaedias are likely to be the most appropriate sources of information to answer their enquiries;**
- **downloading (e.g. by. copying and pasting) text and images from internet sources;**
- **using editing skills to adapt and re-purpose information from websites and/or CD ROMs to suit the needs of different audiences;**
- **evaluating the relevance, accuracy and currency of a website by looking at information such as the web address (e.g. to see if it is an official website);**
- **producing diagrams, plans and maps. Software designed to support such a process, e.g. Local Studies (Soft teach) and Spex+ (Aspex), can greatly assist with this.**

RESPONDING TO E-MAILS

Although reading and responding to e-mails is a relatively straightforward process in terms of both literacy and ICT capabilities, it is mentioned specifically in the National Curriculum documentation for ICT as a requirement and offers particular opportunities for reading (and writing) for meaning. There is very clear guidance on the technicalities of, and health and safety issues related to, the use of e-mails with children, provided on the following websites.

DfES Superhighway safety guidance:
- **http://safety.ngfl.gov.uk/**

Guidance on setting up e-mail projects:
- **www.ictadvice.org.uk/index.php?section=tl&cat=00100100d&rid=465**

Ideas for activities related to the use of e-mail in school and 'safe' sources of e-mail addresses for communicating with other children:
- **http://tlfe.org.uk/ict/email/default.htm**

It is very important that the guidance provided by the DfES and BECTa is followed closely to ensure that children's identities are protected and they develop good, safe working habits and procedures when communicating by e-mail and in other ways via the internet.

The following activities provide some ideas for making effective use of e-mail within the context of English teaching and learning:

Key Stage 1
- **Best done as a whole-class activity initially. There are various e-mail addresses that children can correspond with (e.g.** www.emailsanta.com**) to give them experience of sending and receiving e-mails.**

CLASSROOM STORY

Parents of children in the reception class at Camelsdale First School regularly use e-mail to correspond with the teacher. The teacher encouraged the children to send e-mails telling their parents what they were doing and how much they were enjoying being in school. Eventually, the children were corresponding with family members in other countries and plotting the responses on a world map (see **www.mape.org.uk/curriculum/communications/pdf2.htm***).*

Lower Key Stage 2
- **Interactive uses of e-mail. For example:**
  - **as part of a literacy theme the children could correspond daily with a character in a class book who then replies each evening (i.e. teacher's homework);**
  - **children from one class can correspond with those in another class (in the same or different schools) and write a collaborative story, e.g. by writing alternate sentences in the story (where ICT lessons coincide) or writing alternate paragraphs (when lessons do not coincide). This has been shown to generate considerable enthusiasm and discussion particularly among those who find literacy learning difficult.**

Upper Key Stage 2
- **E-mail projects such as those indicated above can be adapted making the content more appropriate for the needs of older children (e.g. corresponding with an author or seeking information from an organisation to support persuasive writing);**
- **more challenging projects can be organised requiring some setting-up by the teacher. For example:**
  - **the 'Our Day Today' project organised by Brixton Connections saw children from 66 schools across the world providing statistical information and written accounts of one specific day in the life of their school (see** www.brixton-connections.org.uk/ourday.html**);**

CLASSROOM STORY

Children from a Year 5 class in an urban primary school in Ellesmere Port contacted a Year 4 class in a rural school in Cumbria and exchanged information about their localities. In addition to writing and responding to personal e-mails the children gathered data about how they travelled to school, the sorts of shops their parents used and what they did in their leisure time. Although this was primarily a geography topic, the children presented the information using a database, word processor and e-mail package.

- **links to online projects such as these can be found on the ePals website:** www.epals.com/ **or the European Schoolsnet website:** www.eun.org/eun.org2/eun/en/myeurope/content.cfm?lang=en&ov=6516

TEXT MANIPULATION AND PROBLEM-SOLVING PROGRAMS

In addition to drill and practice programs, supporting the development of specific literacy skills and knowledge, and content-free software, such as word processors, there is a range of programs which enable children to exercise and develop literacy skills in problem-solving contexts.

There are several programs available which provide examples and enable teachers to produce on-screen cloze passages. A passage of text is presented with various letters or words omitted. The children need to draw on their knowledge of text to predict the missing words. The advantage of electronic versions over paper-based alternatives is that the computer can provide children with immediate feedback. Some programs enable the teacher to specify acceptable alternatives for missing words, while others provide lists of specific words to be dragged and dropped into the spaces.

'Developing Tray', a text-based problem-solving program which first appeared in the 1970s, has recently been relaunched by 2Simple software and has spawned several derivatives, e.g. Disclose (available free at **www.mape.org.uk/kids/index.htm**). Children are presented with a piece of text with letters and/or punctuation missing. The children are required to complete the missing elements by deducing and predicting the missing letters. Correct predictions earn points, and incorrect 'guesses' lose points. Teachers can enter their own passages of text and decide what proportion of the text or which specific letters are omitted. The most extreme 'problem' initially shows no text or punctuation but merely dashes to indicate the position of letters. In this case the children might predict that a one-letter word is 'a'. If they are correct they can opt to show the position of all the 'a's in the text. They might then predict that a three-letter word beginning with 'a' is 'and', and if they are correct will be shown the position of all the 'n's and 'd's etc. This type of program is highly versatile in that the passages of text can include target word families, rhyming poetry, particular genres of text, etc.

Discloze is available from the MAPE website (www.mape.org.uk)

Another problem-solving activity which requires children to engage closely with text involves the use of databases to solve mysteries or crimes. For example, the children are presented with a newspaper report of a crime and must use the clues in the text to search for the most likely suspects on a database. A good example of this called 'Whodunnit?' is provided free of charge on the MAPE website (**www.mape.org.uk/ kids/index.htm**). Teachers and children can, of course, produce their own databases of villains and crime stories for others to solve.

CLASSROOM STORY

A class of Year 3 and Year 4 children was studying the canal which passed through their locality. They found out that the canals were plagued by thieves. They invented their own villains, made wanted posters and entered their villains' details into a database prepared by the teacher. They each then wrote a newspaper story about a crime committed by their villain containing a partial description (no more than three details). The children then solved each others' crimes by using the database.

Any activity which requires children to search for and locate specific information will enhance reading skills such as skimming and scanning text. While these are best developed in context such as locating information related to a topic being studied, there are occasions when a computer program such as Text Detectives (Sherston) enables the teacher to focus on practising specific techniques for locating text-based information efficiently.

SUMMARY OF KEY POINTS

- **While drill and practice programs can be used to support the development of specific reading skills, they do little to develop ICT capabilities.**

- **Branching stories and simple adventure programs offer considerable potential for developing reading skills as they rely on reading for meaning.**

- **Word-processing tasks can be devised to support reading skill development.**

- **CD ROM encyclopaedias enable children to search and browse for information.**

- **Animated diagrams can help children to understand the relationship between simplified drawings and what they represent.**

- **E-mail activities provide incentives for reluctant readers.**

- **Database activities can be devised to help children identify and extract key information from texts.**

5 ICT and English in the classroom – writing

Inspections have shown for many years that one of the most frequent uses for ICT in the primary classroom is word processing. Teachers, in the main, feel confident in the use of word processors with children, as writing is an important part of most classroom activities. However, since the introduction of the literacy hour, opportunities for children to engage in extended writing activities have diminished and concern has been expressed (e.g. OFSTED, 2002b) about the relative lack of progress in the development of children's written work.

A major disadvantage of using the word processor is the time taken for children to type their own text. At the end of a half-hour session some children may have entered little more than two brief sentences after painstakingly hunting for the relevant keys. While it might be useful for children to be taught touch-typing (indeed, some primary schools do this), most teachers feel that time is better spent in productive use of the computer, with keyboard skills being developed concomitantly through other activities.

While word processing is the most obvious application for ICT in the development of writing, there are other ways in which writing skills can be developed. Furthermore, making use of a word processor for little more than copy-typing work which has already been handwritten makes insufficient use of the facilities offered by most word processors.

The following ICT-based activities offer considerable potential for the development of children's writing abilities.

- **Using drill and practice programs to enhance specific writing skills and knowledge, such as punctuation and spelling.**
- **Using specific programs to reinforce correct letter formation.**
- **Using word processors to assist with:**
  - **composition:**

    developing children's use of vocabulary;

    changing the way an existing piece of work is presented, to give it more impact, for example, or make it easier to read;

    changing the focus of a piece of writing;

    raising awareness of the features of different genres of writing;
  - **planning and drafting:**

    composing, re-drafting, reviewing and editing text;

    using features such as text-to-speech;

  – punctuation:

   exploring the effect of punctuation on meaning;

  – spelling:

   reinforcing knowledge of strategies and morphology;

   the use of spellcheckers and predictive word processors;

  – presentation:

   experimenting with different layouts and formats to evaluate their effectiveness;

   combining text and images to convey information efficiently;

  – awareness of standard English:

   investigating ways of communicating information to different audiences for different purposes;

  – awareness of language structure:

   improving a piece of writing by changing words or phraseology;

   exploring sentence composition.

- Communicating electronically with others via fax, e-mail, web-chat, etc.
- Using ICT tools to assist with the writing process.

USING DRILL AND PRACTICE PROGRAMS

As mentioned previously, drill and practice programs should be used sparingly as they are of limited value in developing children's skills and knowledge unless they are integrated very carefully into a programme of work which links closely to purposeful contexts for the application of the skills being reinforced. Spelling practice programs are seen by teachers to have the greatest impact on English learning in the primary classroom (see Fischer Trust, 2002) and, while they provide opportunities for children to practise spelling, they are really only effective if the word lists are based on a child's recurrent errors and if used to support activities in which the words are being used in the child's written work. An effective way to achieve this is by allowing the children to create their own word lists of 'tricky' words that they want to learn to spell.

PROGRAMS TO REINFORCE CORRECT LETTER FORMATION

As with drill and practice programs, programs which demonstrate the correct formation of letters are best used in conjunction with practical and purposeful activities requiring the use of handwriting. They can be useful, however, in introducing letter formation to groups or the whole class as the animated screens can be appealing and memorable for the children.

Fonts which resemble various handwriting styles are available on the internet (e.g. **http://cgm.cs.mcgill.ca/ ~ luc/kids.html**). These can be very useful for the preparation of activity sheets and worksheets for children, saving considerable time and effort.

ACTIVITIES USING WORD PROCESSORS

The most effective way for children to use word processors in the primary classroom is to draft and edit short, focused pieces of writing such as poetry, wanted posters, letters, paragraphs, descriptions, etc. or to develop a piece of writing which has already been typed in. This could be a chunk of text copied from the internet or a CD ROM package, text scanned in from a book, text typed in by the teacher or a child's own work typed in by the teacher, teaching assistant or parent helper.

Educational word processors offer a number of additional features which are not found on word processors designed for use in an office environment. These include:

- **simplified toolbars and icons;**
- **text-to-speech, whereby letters, syllables, words, sentences and/or passages are read aloud by the computer during or after typing;**
- **word banks, which provide lists of words, phrases or sentences which can be entered into a document by the click of a mouse button;**
- **simple insertion and editing of pictures on screen without the need for complicated tools.**

While the development of skills and knowledge associated with the use of a word processor is to some extent hierarchical (i.e. some skills are easier to acquire than others), it is important that this is not the prime factor driving the choice of activity. What is more significant is the purpose of an activity in terms of a child's or group's literacy learning. Through careful planning and preparation it is possible for children to develop their word-processing ICT capabilities through the completion of interesting and meaningful literacy-based activities.

Sometimes a similar literacy activity might be appropriate for children who have a range of ICT capabilities. For example, the children are presented with a passage of text in which 'nice' is the only adjective. The literacy task is for the children to replace all the occurrences of 'nice' with more interesting and appropriate alternatives. Consider how the level of challenge for this activity can be altered by changing the way it is presented:

Lower Key Stage 1
- **The passage is presented in MS Word or Talking First Word using drop-down form fields. The children click on each occurrence of 'nice' in the text and select the alternatives presented.**

Upper Key Stage 1
- **The children are provided with a list of alternatives for 'nice' in a word bank. They are required to delete each occurrence of 'nice' and click on an alternative in the word bank.**

Lower Key Stage 2
- **A list of alternatives for 'nice' is provided at the top of the page. The children have to delete each occurrence of 'nice', then drag and drop or cut and paste the most appropriate word from the list.**

Upper Key Stage 2

- **The children click on each occurrence of 'nice' and select a synonym using the thesaurus in the tools menu;**

- **as above, but before making their alterations, they turn on the 'track changes' option in MS Word and, when they have amended the passage, they swap with another group to 'accept' or 'reject' each other's changes.**

As can be seen, while the literacy demands of the activity vary only slightly, the level of intellectual challenge and the application of ICT skills varies considerably (see **www.chester.ac.uk/education/primary_resources**). When planning and preparing ICT-based literacy activities the level of challenge and demand needs to be taken into account. Even within the same class, there will be a wide variation in the ICT capabilities of the children which may not correlate with their competence in English.

The following activities are provided as suggestions for ways in which word processors can be used to support or enhance the learning and teaching of different aspects of the writing process. It should be borne in mind that there is considerable overlap between the activities. While an activity might be presented as an idea under one particular heading, with a slight shift of emphasis, or an alteration of the way it is presented, it could be used to assist with the development of a different aspect of writing.

COMPOSITION

As we have seen, the word processor can be used to provide activities at various levels for the development of the children's use of vocabulary by replacing commonplace words with more interesting alternatives. Further ideas for extending children's use of vocabulary include:

- **simplifying a piece of text, for example copying a paragraph from a website and changing some of the words to make it more appropriate for a younger audience (the thesaurus could be used to assist in this process);**

- **enhancing a skeleton text (e.g. a basic story or account) through the addition of suitable adjectives and adverbs and/or changing some ordinary verbs to those which are more expressive;**

- **changing the meaning of a piece of text by finding alternatives for key words. For example, a paragraph from a book describing a cheerful, jolly person could be changed to make the person sound melancholy, devious or evil;**

- **brainstorming to create a bank of words and phrases suggested by the children. A class poem is created using the words and phrases or the word bank is distributed to all children through a network and they create individual poems (or work in pairs). The resulting poems are shared in the plenary to see how the same stimulus has been used in different ways.**

Editing the presentation of a piece of text:

- **Changing the way an existing piece of work is presented to give it more impact or make it easier to read. This could involve reorganising the information to make it more accessible; simplifying the text to make it more readable; elaborating the text to make it more expressive; emboldening, bullet-pointing or adding sub-headings to make it more structured;**
- **changing the focus for a piece of writing: to make it more appropriate for a different audience; to emulate a particular style or genre (e.g. a tabloid newspaper account); to change its viewpoint; to make it more (or less) persuasive; to make it more descriptive; to raise children's awareness of the structure and features of a genre.**

WRITING FRAMES

One of the most effective and versatile ways of using ICT to support the development of children's abilities with composition is the writing frame. A writing frame is a template document to which the children add content. Writing frames provide a structure for children's written work and can introduce conventions such as 'signpost' phrases linking one paragraph to the next. For example, a writing frame for a piece of persuasive writing might comprise:

It is very important for the family that we get a   because

One of the main reasons in favour of a   is .

Another advantage for us in having a   is that

However, you might argue that a   will

Alternatively,

So, in summary, the benefits to us of getting a   are

For younger children or less confident writers, writing frames can be made highly structured, with spaces for individual words (i.e. cloze). For more accomplished writers, writing frames tend to be more open-ended, demonstrating more sophisticated use of language.

The advantage of a writing frame presented as a word processor document is that children can work collaboratively more readily and rework their writing as it progresses. Furthermore, writing tools such as word banks, spellcheckers and thesauri can be used to enhance the content and quality of the final piece.

Writing frames can be prepared by the teacher and saved as template documents, which means the children will not be able to change the original. Templates are also useful in saving time and effort by providing a framework for their written work. For example, if the children are writing letters to authors they could have a template showing the school's logo and address, together with prompts indicating what needs to go where in the letter.

COMMUNICATING ELECTRONICALLY

The rapid rise in the availability and popularity of the internet and mobile phone technology has profoundly affected the ways in which we can communicate. Concerns have been expressed over the impact of e-mail and text messaging on the use of written language, particularly the tendency for words and phrases to be abbreviated. The critics may not have noticed how this has indicated not only the flexibility and adaptability of written language, but also the redundancy and arbitrariness of spelling patterns in English. For example, rmvng th vwls frm wrds ds nt ncssrly ffct yr blty t rd thm.

While text messaging does offer some opportunities to explore aspects of morphology and phonemic awareness, concerns have been expressed over its effect on spelling. Having access to the internet inevitably presents teachers and learners with considerably more potential for developing aspects of writing through communication with a global audience and access to a wide range of resources. Some opportunities include:

- **communicating with real and fictional people via fax, e-mail, web-chat, etc.;**
- **reading and contributing to online stories;**
- **creating web pages to communicate information and ideas.**

E-mail
In the early days of the National Grid for Learning (NGfL) it was announced that within two years all children would have their own e-mail addresses within school. While those of us who use e-mail on a daily basis appreciate this can be a mixed blessing, it readily became apparent that this option posed more threats to children than opportunities. The DfES website for Superhighway Safety (**http://safety.ngfl.gov.uk**) provides detailed and sound guidance on the precautions teachers must take in using e-mail with children, particularly in protecting their identities and minimising their exposure to risk. However, provided safeguards are taken and parents are informed about the precautions taken and the educational purposes in using e-mail, then a number of interesting and valuable activities can be planned to develop children's writing skills and knowledge in purposeful contexts:

- **communicating with fictional characters;**
- **writing collaborative stories;**
- **exchanging information with e-pals;**
- **seeking information from 'experts';**

- **participating in local, national and international online projects;**
- **reinforcing home/school links.**

COMMUNICATING WITH FICTIONAL CHARACTERS

CLASSROOM STORY

A class of Year 3 children was reading Room on the Broom *(Donaldson, 2001) as their class text. The teacher set up a hotmail account for the witch and the children sent her e-mails asking about her adventures and giving her advice on staying out of trouble. The teacher responded to the children's e-mails in the evenings, establishing a dialogue between the witch and groups of children. The first e-mail was sent as the result of a shared writing activity with the whole class. Subsequent e-mails were composed collaboratively in groups as a guided writing activity, with a different group responding to the witch's reply each day. The teacher was able to use the 'witch's' responses to steer the focus for daily writing.*

WRITING COLLABORATIVE STORIES

CLASSROOM STORY

The teacher of a class of Year 3/Year 4 children was concerned about their inability to work collaboratively. Her attempts to set up conventional group writing activities invariably resulted in arguments or domination and subservience by those concerned. With a parallel class, she set up collaborative writing through e-mail. Each group was paired with another in the parallel class and took turns to write the next sentence in a story. For the first time, the teacher found that most of the groups worked collaboratively, reading the parallel group's contribution, discussing what should happen next, composing the next sentence on screen, checking it, sending it off and waiting excitedly for the reply. Although the stories were inevitably brief and sometimes slightly disjointed, the enthusiasm for writing and collaboration which this activity generated was, she felt, more important than the content of the stories.

This activity is an example of the synchronous use of internet communication. The children were engaging in a dialogue in real time: the equivalent of a conversation. A great advantage of e-mail is the asynchronous nature of its communication. A message or reply can be sent at a time convenient to the sender — invaluable when the correspondents are in different time zones.

EXCHANGING INFORMATION WITH E-PALS

As has been indicated above (see Reading section), finding e-pals in a different part of the country or a different part of the world is relatively straightforward, provided it is done via personal contacts or reputable organisations.

While informal dialogue with an e-pal can be beneficial in developing aspects of writing, it is more interesting and effective if the communication forms part of a larger project to find general and specific information about the life, interests and culture of the other person.

PARTICIPATING IN LOCAL, NATIONAL AND INTERNATIONAL ONLINE PROJECTS

Projects can be set up informally between two teachers, for example two newly qualified teachers who trained together but who have now moved to different parts of the country. A project could initially be established to compare two contrasting localities as part of the geography curriculum. In addition to comparing statistical information about the localities, individual e-pals in the two classes could exchange information about their lifestyles, interests and leisure pursuits.

Local projects are sometimes set up by: secondary schools and feeder primary schools; local education authorities; metropolitan area networks which provide online resources for clusters of schools; or by local organisations and charities interested in working with informal clusters of schools.

National and international projects are continually being introduced and developed. These are often advertised in the educational press or can be found by searching the internet for online school projects. Another source of information for online projects is the British Education and Communication Technology Agency's (BECTa) website (**www.becta.org.uk**) or the European Schoolnet's website (**www.eun.org**). Alternatively, projects can often be accessed by subscribing to an online educational service provider.

SEEKING INFORMATION FROM 'EXPERTS'

Information-handling skills not only include the extraction of information from texts but also from video, CD ROM, the internet and other sources, which can include consulting an expert. This might involve setting up an interview (see Chapter 3) or contacting a well-informed person by post or e-mail. Many websites for organisations include e-mail address links which can be used to contact an enquiries desk or sometimes an individual. Furthermore, university and college websites usually include contact lists, as academics are used to responding to enquiries via e-mail. In the main, people are more responsive to e-mails than to letters. Composing an e-mail to ensure that the information or view sought meets the needs of the topic being studied and is meaningful to the recipient requires the children to be succinct, polite and pointed – in other words, to use written language effectively.

REINFORCING HOME/SCHOOL LINKS

Many homes now have access to the internet. Some primary teachers communicate information to parents about the topics being studied through the school's website and some even use the web to set homework for the children, though there are issues of inclusion inherent in making this the primary means of communication. However, e-mail and the web provide resources and information for those wishing to support their children's learning outside school and for parents and children to communicate with teachers.

The greatest value in reinforcing home/school links must surely lie in the publication of children's work on school websites. This not only provides existing parents with an over-view of the quality of work the children are producing but also acts as a showcase for potential parents and provides children with a boost to their self-esteem.

READING AND CONTRIBUTING TO ONLINE STORIES

The best-known online story is probably *The Never Ending Tale* (**www.coder.com/ creations/tale/**) which is typical of this type of resource. As anyone with access to the internet can contribute to the story, the quality of writing is quite variable, but it can act as a stimulus. For example, it could form the focus for a shared writing session in which the class works together on their contribution, adopting the style of the author of their current class text.

The emulation of this type of story using the school's network, intranet or their internet site offers even greater potential. Different classes or groups of children within a class could contribute instalments to the story in turn, maybe presenting the next contributor with a difficult problem to solve, or introducing a new character/setting in order to shift the focus of the story.

Some websites provide a platform for the publication of children's written work (e.g. Kidpub – **www.kidpub.org/kidpub/**). The ease with which websites can be created makes these sites less necessary than previously but they can act as an incentive to children to develop their written work for a far wider audience than if a story or poem had been confined to an exercise book or posted on the classroom wall.

CREATING WEB PAGES TO COMMUNICATE INFORMATION AND IDEAS

While the publication of written work is useful in rewarding children's efforts or in encouraging children to consider the quality of their work, designing and creating web pages offers even greater opportunities for children to consider the impact of their work on an audience. A website is like no other document because:

- **it is designed specifically to be presented on a computer screen;**
- **it can incorporate text, images, sounds, animations and video clips;**
- **it will have an immediate guaranteed worldwide audience;**
- **there is no intermediary between the creator of the web page and the readers (i.e. there is no censorship or editorial control).**

The technical skills involved in creating a web page are little different from those needed for using a word processor. In fact, most word processors (including MS Word and TextEase) can be used to create web pages. However, considerable thought should be given when designing web pages, as the most effective are those which balance the use of presentational devices with the content to ensure that the information presented makes the best use of the computer screen.

ACTIVITY

Think for a moment about websites you have visited recently, particularly those from which you wanted to discover information about a specific topic. List the features on the web pages which you felt were most helpful and those which were least useful to you.

Some web pages will have presented you with dense blocks of text which needed to be scrolled through; at the other extreme, some web pages will have been no more than a single screen with animated images and a few buttons. In designing a web page, the children will need to consider not only how text will be used to convey information but how it should be presented: whether pictures, photos and diagrams will be useful in conveying information, which sounds and animation could help in making the information clear and if links to other pages or other people's websites ought to be included for those seeking more detailed information.

The design and realisation of websites is a topic beyond the scope of this slim volume, but useful guidance is provided on the BECTa ICT Advice website (**www.ictadvice.org.uk/index.php?section=te&cat=008000&rid=3478&wn=1**) and there are numerous books and other websites providing advice and information on effective (and poor) web design.

Some of the ways in which the creation of web pages could enhance learning and teaching of English include:

- **a platform for celebrating and sharing children's creative writing;**
- **information about the school and its events (e.g. match reports, educational visit accounts, invitations to the school's open day, summer fair, drama production, religious festival, etc.);**
- **an information source about the locality;**
- **an information source about an aspect of the children's other studies (e.g. famous artworks, historical research, mathematical investigations, habitats, weather studies, etc.);**
- **an online questionnaire related to the children's ongoing studies.**

ICT offers children and teachers considerable potential in developing knowledge and skills in the use of language and the communication of information in a range of different forms. Often, the greatest inhibiting factor to the use of ICT in the classroom is not the children or the technology, it is the confidence and knowledge of the teacher. By trying things out, learning from mistakes and building on successes you will come to find approaches which suit your teaching styles and the needs of the children.

SUMMARY OF KEY POINTS

- **Word-processing activities with the same literacy objectives can be varied to develop a range of ICT skills.**
- **Writing frames are versatile resources for developing both literacy and ICT skills and knowledge.**
- **E-mail and web authoring activities offer considerable potential for writing for different audiences.**
- **Health and safety guidance should be followed before using e-mail or creating web pages.**

6 Supporting teaching in primary English with ICT

The previous chapters focused on the opportunities afforded by ICT to support, enhance and, at times, transform pupils' learning in English. This chapter examines ways in which ICT can be used to facilitate, augment or improve teaching. Whereas the previous chapter focused on the child and learning, this chapter concentrates on the teacher and teaching materials.

Teachers could make use of ICT in the following ways:

- **to help with the research, planning and preparation of information and materials for teaching;**
- **to act as a teaching aid supporting their classroom teaching;**
- **to assist with assessment, record-keeping and analysis of children's progress;**
- **to support the teacher's wider professional role through assisting with administrative tasks and professional development.**

All of these are relevant to the teaching of English and, as we have seen already, if used wisely ICT can not only make a positive contribution to children's learning, it can ease the workload of teachers.

USING ICT TO ASSIST WITH PLANNING AND PREPARATION

Planning and preparation for teaching English entails, among other things, the following:

- **background research into the topics being covered;**
- **planning activities to meet the needs of the children and the curriculum;**
- **preparing resource materials to support teaching and learning in the activities planned.**

ICT has a part to play in all the above activities and, provided it is used appropriately, can enhance the quality of your planning and preparation and the effectiveness of your teaching.

BACKGROUND RESEARCH

No matter which subject is being taught, teachers need to research background information about the topics they are teaching. In English, this might include checking up on the correct use of grammatical terms or English usage, but might equally require searching for information about authors, poets, genres or the origin of words and phrases. Similarly, teachers might wish to search for pieces of text and/or pictures related to a topic for use with their children. The internet provides instantaneous access to a wealth of information (see Chapter 7 for information about copyright).

Although using search engines and online directories such as Google and Yahoo! can be very productive, it can be very time-consuming locating the specific information required. A more time-effective approach is to use lists of web links provided by others. Chapter 8 provides an overview of some of these sources with particular reference to those which list specific information related to the teaching of English.

Professional English and educational organisations, such as the UK Reading Association (UKRA) similarly provide information and resources relevant for teaching primary English and many also provide lists of links to other selected websites. Again, refer to Chapter 8 for a comprehensive list.

Trainee teachers and teachers are often concerned about finding appropriate software and ICT-based resources to support their teaching as well as ideas for making effective use of ICT in their teaching. Books such as this can provide an outline of the sorts of activities which are appropriate and suggest types of software which might be relevant and occasionally mention some by name but it is not possible to provide a comprehensive list of all the software which is available. One of the greatest difficulties with ICT is the frequency with which new resources are developed and the rapidity with which materials become dated. No doubt, by the time this book is published, some of the web links which are listed in the final chapter will have changed. However, it is remarkable how resilient some educational software can be. For example, Granny's Garden (4mation) was developed in the early days of the micro computers for schools programme in the early 1980s and is still going strong now (though in a modified form). Many other programs fall into this category. As mentioned by Bennett and Pearson (2002), it is surprising and disappointing how few of the more recently developed educational programs have made full use of the technology which is available.

To find out more about educational software appropriate for English, refer to the sources set out in Chapter 8.

PLANNING ACTIVITIES

ICT can assist teachers with planning for English teaching through:

- the use of template documents such as medium-term planning grids and lesson planning templates;
- the ability of a word processor to copy and paste information from one document to another;
- the provision of lesson plans and ideas for activities via the internet.

PLANNING TEMPLATES

Template documents are very easy to produce with a word processor such as MS Word. Not only does this speed up the planning process for teachers, it ensures that the quality of presentation of the information is sufficiently high for others to be able to read and make sense of them. This can be useful when other teachers take over a class (e.g. supply teachers or the headteacher covering for absence) but also if planning is shared with parents. The headteachers of some schools 'publish' teachers' medium-term planning on their websites for parents to refer to.

DOCUMENT SHARING

Being able to copy learning outcomes from documents such as the *National Literacy Strategy* or the *QCA Scheme of Work for ICT* can greatly speed up the planning process, particularly where teachers have to adapt the content to suit the needs of their children. All curricular documents are available via the internet and hence accessible for adaptation in this way.

Accessing others' lesson plans and ideas

The National Grid for Learning (NGfL) was introduced amid a blaze of publicity in 1997. The principal purposes of the NGfL are to:

- *provide a national focus and agenda for harnessing new technologies to raise educational standards … especially the new literacy and numeracy targets.*
- *Remove barriers to learning, ensuring opportunities and access for all, including those in isolated areas and those with special needs.*
- *Provide high quality software, content and services which are relevant and differentiated according to needs.*

DFEE (1997, p. 3)

The first of these aims is part of an ongoing process. Through the Virtual Teachers' Centre (**www.vtc.ngfl.gov.uk**) and the Teachers' Resource Exchange (**http:// tre.ngfl. gov.uk/**) information, lesson plans, ideas, resources and teaching materials are available for use by teachers. As with any resource, its effectiveness is dependent on:

- **the quality and range of information available;**
- **the appropriateness of the information;**
- **the ease with which information can be located and accessed;**
- **the ability of the teachers accessing the information to make effective use of it in the classroom.**

The number and range of resources is steadily increasing as teachers and developers add materials. As the quantity increases so does the time taken to locate and access the information that a teacher might need. Inevitably, lesson plans may have to be adapted for use with a particular group of children or to suit the teaching styles of the teacher intending to use them. Often, it might prove quicker for teachers to produce their own plans than spend time searching for the particular idea appropriate their needs. However, such information can be extremely useful when looking for new ideas especially when teaching a topic for the first time.

Dotted around the country are local NGfLs, such as the Northern Grid for Learning (**www.northerngrid.co.uk/**), the Kent National Grid for Learning (**www.kented. org.uk/ngfl/**) and the Birmingham Grid for Learning (**www.bgfl.org/bgfl.portal/**). These offer the same range of facilities as the NGfL but are more relevant to the schools, teachers, children and curricular topics of the locality they serve.

In addition to the 'official' NGfL websites there are a number of other websites offering free resource materials, lesson plans, ideas and information for primary teachers (see Chapter 8 for a comprehensive list). Many of these have been accredited by the NGfL. Again, the quality and range is variable and time is needed to locate exactly what is needed.

PREPARING TEACHING AND LEARNING MATERIALS

This section deals with resources which are prepared by the teacher for use by children working in groups or independently. The teaching materials and resources for these purposes fall into the following categories:

- **paper-based resources, such as worksheets, writing frames, handouts and guidance notes;**
- **computer-based resources produced by the teacher (e.g. e-worksheets, template documents, interactive quizzes, software files);**
- **commercial computer-based resources (e.g. online activities, computer programs).**

PAPER-BASED RESOURCES

While book-based and commercial photocopiable materials are used extensively in classrooms teachers often augment these with worksheets and handouts they have produced. The budget for photocopying in schools has risen steadily since these machines were introduced. Primary teachers recognise the importance of providing children with attractively presented materials to stimulate interest and to exemplify the quality of response they are expecting.

Most teachers are quite adept at using word processors and desktop publishing packages such as Publisher (Microsoft) to produce work for children. These can be greatly enhanced by the addition of suitable clip art. In addition to general clip art provided on CD ROMs, most pictures available on websites can be copied by clicking the right-hand mouse button (or holding the mouse button down on an Apple or iMac). Some publishers provide CD ROMs with clip-art images of the characters in their reading schemes for teachers to add to their own worksheets or web-based resources.

The NGfL and the other sources mentioned above not only provide lesson plans over the internet, they also include downloadable classroom resources, mostly produced by teachers. You will need to balance the time taken to locate and adapt the worksheet you need with the time it might take you to produce one of your own. Sometimes, however, a day spent trawling websites for resources which might be needed over the coming half-term can yield dividends in the savings made in preparation time.

COMPUTER-BASED RESOURCES

With a minimum of additional effect, most paper-based resources can be presented as computer-based activities. Because most young children do not have accomplished typing skills, there is seldom sufficient time in a lesson for them to create a document of any length. It is important therefore that teachers prepare tasks, framework files or partially completed documents for them to complete.

E-WORKSHEETS

At its most basic level an e-worksheet is a computer version of a paper-based worksheet. An individual or small group of children completes the activity on-screen using a word processor while the rest of the children complete the paper-based version. This provides ICT-inexperienced children with valuable hands-on experience, but can also help those lacking in confidence in English to make use of some of the word processor's tools such as spellchecking or text-to-speech.

With slight adaptation, the same worksheet could include additional features such as drop-down form fields (available in MS Word), word banks (available in Clicker, FreeText and TextEase), or hidden prompts such as buttons and hyperlinks giving guidance or hints on how to complete the activity. In this way, one root worksheet could be differentiated to provide extra support or additional challenge.

SKELETON TEXTS

The most basic skeleton test is a cloze passage, with missing words for the children to complete. A computer-based version could include missing words in a word bank or as a list to be cut and pasted or dragged and dropped into place. A writing frame is another, more extreme, skeleton text (see opposite). Another form of skeleton text is one which includes bland sentences outlining a story or event, or describing an object, person or place which the children must enhance. A skeleton text may range from a single sentence to the bare bones of a complete account or short story awaiting embellishment. Another form of skeleton text is a series of words and phrases which could have arisen from suggestions by the children in a previous brainstorming lesson.

CLASSROOM STORY

A class of Year 6 children was asked by the teacher to jot down a series of words and phrases describing the downpour of rain they had just experienced. The children were then invited by the teacher to share their best two or three words or phrases. She typed these into a word processor. The resulting file was then saved on the school's network as a skeleton document which the children opened on their own computers in the computer suite. In pairs, they edited the words and phrases to produce their own expressive poetry based on the original word list. (See next page.)

QUIZZES AND CHECK TESTS

Simple tests and quizzes can be devised quickly by teachers using freeware programs such as Webquestions, Hot potatoes or Quiz maker which are available via the internet (see Chapter 8). It is also possible for teachers to devise and produce their own interactive resources using presentation software such as PowerPoint, multimedia software such as Illuminatus or HyperStudio, or even some word processors which include hyperlinking such as MS Word and TextEase. However, the educational benefits to the children are seldom worth the effort spent in producing this type of resource. It would be far more time-effective to produce e-worksheets or writing frames.

torrential	spluttering	spluttering guttering
downpour	gushing	gulping down the drain
deluge	rushing water	
cloud-burst	cascading down from the sky	drain
cascade	pouring	grid
drizzle	roaring	downspout
mist	flowing	gutter
shower	streaming	guttering
	flooding	puddle
slipping and sliding	floating	sewer
lashing at my face	foaming	watercourse
trickling down my neck	splashing	
soaked to the skin	slashing down	*like ....*
drenched	gulping	needles
sopping wet	squirting	thin glass rods
	spurting	spears
damp	overflowing	arrows falling
dank	spattering	daggers
sodden	trickling	cats and dogs
humid	dripping	
moist	dribbling	
	oozing	
whipping	spewing	
slithering	spilling	

Rain

Pouring
Roaring
Streaming from the sky
Gushing
Rushing
Slashing down on me
Needles prick me
Daggers stab me
Spears pierce through me
As I splash my way to school
Gutters splutter
Downspouts stutter
Water pours from every nook and cranny
Streams trickle down my nose
Rivers tumble down my neck
Waterfalls cascade down my back
Like a waterlogged dog
I stagger into school
Steaming and dripping on the mat
I love the rain
Sometimes

Duncan (Year 6)

COMMERCIALLY PRODUCED COMPUTER-BASED RESOURCES

Increasingly, independent suppliers are providing web-based resources through annual subscription (e.g. Espresso Education). In addition to online activities designed to support specific aspects of learning in English and other subjects, opportunities are created for schools to work collaboratively and gain access to technical guidance and support (though this varies between providers). Most of these online suppliers provide opportunities for potential customers to try out some of their resources for free (e.g. **www.thebigbus.com/free/resources/writing/index.htm**) to give you some idea of what is available. Many of the activities for English fall into the drill and practice category aimed at supporting the teaching and learning of a quite specific range of skills and knowledge (e.g. word sorting, cloze, sound-matching). The opportunities for building online learning communities through these portals and extending the range of learning opportunities seem restrictive with all but a few of these providers at present, though this may change in the course of time.

ICT AS A TEACHING AID

The *National Literacy Strategy* (DfEE, 1998) recommends that the daily hour-long literacy lesson should be divided into four clear sections:

- *Shared text work* (a balance of reading and writing) with the whole class – 15 minutes.
- *Focused word* (Key Stage 1) *or word and sentence* (Key Stage 2) *work* with the whole class – 15 minutes.
- *Independent reading, writing or word work* while the teacher works with at least one (Key Stage 2) or two (Key Stage 1) ability groups on guided text work – 20 minutes.
- *A whole-class plenary* reviewing, reflecting, consolidating teaching points and presenting work covered in the lesson – 10 minutes.

The structure for the literacy hour is not statutory but most teachers have adopted organisational approaches which incorporate key features of the framework in their teaching.

Whole-class teaching

It is significant that the recommendation is for the majority of the hour (40 minutes) to be spent in whole-class teaching activities. The rationale is that the effective learning takes place under the direct control of the teacher. Research has shown (e.g. Wragg et *al.*, 1998) that, almost without exception, effective teachers make good use of plenary sessions at the end of their lessons to consolidate and assess the children's learning.

ICT can be used to enhance the quality of whole-class teaching by careful use of hardware (equipment) and software (programs).

HARDWARE

As with any performance, whole-class teaching relies on all members of the audience being able to see and hear what is going on. While it is possible for a class of very young children to be grouped around a large monitor screen, it is inadequate for most

Key Stage 2 classes simply because the children are larger and those at the back would be unable to read what is on the screen.

- **It is possible to connect a computer to more than one monitor screen. This might prove useful for special projects or when monitors can be fixed in place around the classroom. Very large (e.g. 42-inch) screen displays can be purchased, flat-screen plasma displays being the most desirable. However, these are extremely expensive and unwieldy to manoeuvre from room to room.**

- **Data projectors are also relatively expensive (approximately three times the cost of a desktop computer) but offer a flexible means of enabling large groups of children to see the screen simultaneously. Many are lightweight and highly portable. It should be borne in mind that although the bulbs for these projectors are usually guaranteed for around three years' use, replacements cost in the region of £300–£500. Furthermore, the intensity of the light produced by these projectors can cause permanent damage to the retina by looking into the lens for as little as five seconds. Projectors should therefore be positioned outside the normal eye-line and teachers should avoid standing in the beam while addressing the class.**

- **Although interactive whiteboards are becoming more common in primary classrooms, they are by no means ubiquitous. They require a large screen display such as that provided by a plasma screen or a data projector. The screen on to which the image is projected is touch-sensitive and hence the computer can be controlled through the use of a special stylus or pen (or, with some models, the pressure of a finger). Interactive whiteboards offer a range of resources which can be used to enhance teaching by enabling the teacher and the children to interact with text and objects in full view of the whole class.**

When used with a projector or large monitor, cordless keyboards and mice provide an alternative method of enabling children and the teacher to control the computer. The mouse and/or keyboard can be passed to particular children to click on on-screen buttons or to edit and enter text.

SOFTWARE

In theory, any piece of relevant software can be used for whole-class teaching in English. For example, you might want to demonstrate how to use a CD ROM encyclopaedia or an internet search engine to teach information-handling skills such as the use of key words for narrowing down a search, skimming and scanning pages for information or using the 'find on page' option for locating a specific word or phrase.

However, word processors, multimedia authoring packages and presentation software provide opportunities for you as a teacher to prepare specifically targeted activities to introduce, emphasise, reinforce or revise particular concepts, knowledge or skills.

USING WORD PROCESSORS FOR WHOLE-CLASS TEACHING

As we have seen in the previous chapter, word processors offer considerable potential for developing aspects of children's learning in English. Many of the activities mentioned pre-viously can be adapted for use in whole-class teaching but the following ideas are offered as suggestions about how the features offered by a word processor can be used specifically to teach aspects of English:

- *Highlighting, text colour and emphasis* – word processors such as **MS Word** include facilities to highlight chunks of text. At a basic level, words or phrases can be emboldened or changed in colour to draw attention to them. **MS Word** has a highlighter pen tool for emphasising blocks of text. These features could be used to identify parts of speech (e.g. highlighting all nouns in red and adjectives in green) or showing all occurrences of direct speech and so on. Passages of text can be created with the text colour of strategic words or phrases changed to match the page colour, effectively making them invisible. The missing words can be revealed by highlighting and/or changing the text colour or the background colour.

- *Search and replace* – the search and replace function can be used to work through a passage of text replacing all occurrences of a familiar word (such as 'nice') with more expressive alternatives. A skeleton text could be prepared which includes the word 'adjective' at strategic points and the children are required to substitute these with appropriate words.

- *Moving text* – being able to cut and paste and/or drag and drop words or pieces of text without the need for handling fiddly pieces of paper or sticky-notes opens up all manner of possibilities for sequencing words, sentences or paragraphs, for text-level work in completing writing frames, or for shared writing activities such as editing a passage to make it more readable.

- *Zooming-in on text or enlarging font size* – this is particularly valuable when attempting whole-class teaching with a monitor rather than a projected display or plasma screen. This approach could be used for shared reading or writing tasks, such as focusing on the use of punctuation.

- *Inserting text* – The ease with which text can be inserted with a word processor offers considerable potential for shared writing. For example, a skeleton text can be enhanced through the addition of more detail such as the insertion of adjectives and adverbs or the elaboration of descriptions. Furthermore, the use of template documents such as writing frames can help to emphasise the content, structure and layout of particular genres.

- *Deleting text* – Deletion offers opportunities for text to be simplified or summarised. For example, a passage of text copied from the internet can be reduced to a series of bullet-pointed statements conveying the key information.

- *Formatting text* – The impact on the audience of different formats and presentations can be achieved through the addition of paragraphs, headings, bullet points, tables and columns, emboldening, etc. For example, a block of descriptive prose can be reformatted into a shaped poem or key descriptions in an information text can be sorted into a table.

- *Entering text* – the greatest potential that ICT offers to whole-class teaching lies in shared writing. It is possible for an entire piece of writing to be constructed collaboratively, but this tends to be very time-consuming. Hence it is more effective to develop an existing document or compose something using a writing frame or template document.

- *Language tools* – spellchecking and the thesaurus facility can be used for vocabulary development. For example, spelling mistakes in everyday words in a passage of text can be corrected or substituted on-screen, with children selecting the most appropriate alternatives. Similarly, the word count facility can be used to help summarise a piece of text to a given word limit or to compose a message or small ad with the minimum of words.

As can be seen, the great virtue of using ICT for whole-class teaching lies in the opportunities it provides for emphasising publicly the key features of text and enabling the children to contribute ideas.

USING PRESENTATION AND MULTIMEDIA AUTHORING SOFTWARE FOR WHOLE-CLASS TEACHING

Presentation software was originally developed to emulate photographic and overhead projection slides used to illustrate formal presentations such as the delivery of a conference paper or a talk in a business meeting. Hence, the software enables the user to design a series of screens or 'slides' for presentation in sequence. Various effects can be added to slides such as animations, sounds and transitions between slides. While presentation software is designed principally to show slides in a linear sequence, some presentation programs also include the facility to add hyperlinks and buttons. These can be programmed to respond when clicked by making sounds, moving a particular slide, opening a web page, loading a document, opening another program or starting a video clip. These features are also provided by multimedia authoring packages which might include additional functions such as giving feedback when dragging and dropping objects correctly or creating more sophisticated animated scenes.

Presentation and multimedia programs offer a range of opportunities for whole-class teaching aspect of English, such as the following.

Word level:

- **Parts of words (e.g. phonemes, syllables, onsets, rimes, blends, digraphs, suffixes, prefixes) can be added or highlighted by moving from one slide to the next. Their appearance (or disappearance) can be animated to emphasise their place in the word or extracted and sorted into families.**
- **Letters, syllables, phonemes, endings, blends, etc. can be dragged and dropped to break down or build words.**
- **Words can be dragged and dropped to be sorted into rhyming or analogous spelling 'families'.**
- **Hidden buttons can be positioned behind target words to respond when clicked (e.g. to emphasise target phonemes/graphemes).**

Sentence level

- **Punctuation can be made to appear (or disappear) by moving from one slide to the next (i.e. the two slides are identical apart from the punctuation marks which can be animated maybe with the addition of distinctive sound effects).**

- Words (e.g. verbs, adjectives, rhymes) can be made to spiral into sentences, change colour or disappear to emphasise their contribution or to reinforce their identification.
- Words can be dragged and dropped to compose new sentences, to explore the restructuring of sentences or to sequence words.
- Hidden buttons can be positioned behind words to respond when clicked, e.g. to name the word or to 'read' aloud a phrase or completed sentence.
- Punctuation marks can be animated to appear on command or change colour to indicate their position or function.

Text level

- Key words or phrases can be highlighted, animated or extracted.
- Hidden buttons or links can be added to specific sections of a passage so that when clicked words are highlighted or changed (e.g. connectives change colour, high frequency words are emboldened ready for replacement, key phrases are extracted for closer inspection on a new slide).
- Sentences or paragraphs can be dragged and dropped for sequencing.

USING ICT FOR PERSONAL AND PROFESSIONAL DEVELOPMENT

Since the introduction of the National Curriculum, SATs, OFSTED inspections, the National Literacy Strategy and league tables, the pressure on schools and teachers for accountability has steadily increased. Teachers increasingly need to ensure they have up-to-date information about legislation, trends in teaching, their children's progress and ideas to enhance the quality of their teaching. Fortunately, this increase in accountability has coincided with an unprecedented rise in the availability of ICT resources in schools and the development of the internet.

ICT can be used to support professional development and administrative tasks related to the teaching of English through:

- **access to topical information about education;**
- **increased opportunities for communication with colleagues, parents and outside agencies;**
- **software tools to assist with the preparation of teaching materials;**
- **software tools to assist with the recording and analysis of pupils' progress.**

ACCESS TO INFORMATION

Chapter 8 includes the web addresses of most of the government agencies and indepen-dent organisations which provide guidance, advice and information on the teaching of English. For guidance on making effective use of ICT in teaching, the most useful website is that provided by BECTa (the British Educational and Communications Technology Agency). They provide guidance materials, information sheets and links related to most educational aspects of ICT usage.

INCREASED OPPORTUNITIES FOR COMMUNICATION

As has been mentioned in previous chapters, there will be occasions when children want to ask an expert for advice or information — the same is equally true for teachers. Accessing websites might provide ideas for teaching a topic but, from time to time, specific information might be required, particularly if the enquiry stems from some ongoing work, a difficulty which has arisen in the classroom or an issue to which there seem to be conflicting answers.

The Virtual Teachers' Centre (**www.vtc.ngfl.gov.uk**) hosts a number of discussion forums on various themes. A question posted on such a forum will produce a number of responses from colleagues who have faced and overcome the same sort of problem.

In Chapter 5, there is reference to a reception class teacher who makes regular use of e-mail to correspond with parents. In addition to e-mail as a means of communication, many schools post information to parents on their websites and some teachers even set homework tasks for the children to complete during holiday periods by posting the materials on their classroom website.

SOFTWARE TOOLS FOR PREPARING TEACHING MATERIALS

Chapters 3, 4 and 5 provide a range of ideas for making use of software tools such as word processors, presentation packages and multimedia to prepare and present teaching materials. In Chapter 8 are listed websites offering ready-made lesson plans and teaching materials. In addition, there are websites and CD ROMs devoted to the provision of template worksheets and resources such as child-related clip art. Some websites include free downloadable resources such as the quiz-making program provided by MAPE (Micros and Primary Education — **www.mape.org.uk**). Browsing software catalogues or visiting suppliers' websites will yield a range of other utility programs to assist you in the production of classroom materials.

SOFTWARE TOOLS FOR RECORDING AND ANALYSING PROGRESS

The most straightforward form of ICT-based record-keeping is a paper-based mark list using a table produced in a word processor. This approach can be used to record the children's results on a computer but is restricted when it comes to analysis. A more effective method is to create a similar table as a spreadsheet. Once the results have been entered, formulae can be used to automatically calculate totals and averages and standardise scores. Some spreadsheets (e.g. MS Excel) enable you to highlight cells in particular ways to show when scores are within certain bands. Results can also be presented as graphs to help spot trends or persistent patterns. It is also possible for scores to be merged into word-processed documents to, for example, produce individualised letters or reports to parents.

There are software packages which are specifically designed to record, analyse and present results and others to help draw up IEPs (Individual Education Plans) for those with Special Educational Needs (SENs). Again, consulting suppliers' websites or catalogues will provide you with information about these products.

SUMMARY OF KEY POINTS

- The internet can assist with background research and provide resources, including lesson plans for teachers.

- ICT resources are particularly useful for whole-class teaching activities which form a major part of the literacy hour.

- Teachers can prepare their own resources for use with interactive whiteboards using word processors and presentation packages. These can later be used by children for independent work.

- Word processors are particularly effective for shared writing activities – even without an interactive whiteboard.

- The most efficient way to produce resources for independent work in the literacy hour is to adapt a printed worksheet as a computer-based activity.

7 Managing ICT when teaching English

Many teachers find the integration of ICT activities into their classroom teaching difficult. An increase in the number of schools moving their computers into suites has meant that, whereas in the past teachers might assign a group to a computer-based task as part of a subject lesson, for some this option is now no longer available. Pressures from SATs preparation, league tables and the introduction of the literacy hour with its emphasis on whole-class teaching have further squeezed the time and opportunities available for children to engage in sustained hands-on computer-based activities related to English. However, as mentioned in Chapter 1, teachers are finding ways of organising their time and resources to develop pupils' ICT capabilities within the context of purposeful English lessons.

The management of ICT, as with any curriculum area, requires the teacher to organise a combination of factors:

- **managing the curriculum;**
- **managing assessment and record keeping;**
- **managing time;**
- **managing resources;**
- **managing people.**

Unlike most curriculum subjects, ICT is not only taught in discrete ICT lessons, it is integrated across all areas of the primary school curriculum. In any one week a class of children might use or have contact with ICT in five or six subject areas in addition to an hour-long ICT lesson in the school's computer suite. Ensuring that all these disparate pieces coalesce into a well-organised, integrated and cohesive programme of study is the responsibility of the teacher. So how might this be achieved and how do we ensure that the aspects of ICT which the children encounter as part of their English lessons form part of a coherent whole?

MANAGING THE CURRICULUM

As has been mentioned in Chapter 1, incorporating ICT activities into English lessons requires a working knowledge and understanding of:

- **the requirements for the Foundation Stage curriculum (where applicable);**
- **the National Curriculum requirements for English;**
- **the National Curriculum requirements for ICT;**
- **the National Literacy Strategy;**
- **the school's schemes of work for ICT and English;**
- **the children's past experiences and attainment in English and ICT.**

The National Curriculum for English and the National Literacy Strategy mention ICT but do not specify precisely how children should use ICT. The National Curriculum requirements for ICT are written in general terms and hence do not specify which aspects of

ICT should be taught in which subject areas. Furthermore, the QCA Scheme of Work for ICT, which is followed by many primary schools with varying degrees of rigour, does not indicate specific subject contexts for the activities, though a recently introduced supplement (DfES/QCA, 2003) does suggest a range of subject-focused integrated tasks which could be incorporated into the various units. English-based activities are described for:

- **Unit ID – Labelling and classifying;**
- **Unit 2A – Writing stories;**
- **Unit 2C – Finding information;**
- **Unit 3A – Combining text and graphics;**
- **Unit 3D – Using e-mail;**
- **Unit 4A – Writing for different audiences;**
- **Unit 6A – Multimedia presentation.**

However, the document does indicate that other units could be adapted by a teacher for use within a subject context. The great advantage of English is that, like ICT, it has a cross-curricular application; aspects of English can be developed within any subject.

The secret for the successful integration of ICT into subject teaching lies in the quality of a teacher's medium-term planning. Without a carefully structured and considered medium-term plan, the various ICT activities which occur in the course of a placement, half-term or term tend to become isolated and disjointed.

To ensure that ICT planning takes account of subject contexts the following approach can be adopted:

- **identify the ICT focus for the medium term planning period;**
- **define a series of learning outcomes/objectives for the period;**
- **draw up subject plans, identifying opportunities for meeting the ICT learning outcomes;**
- **complete the ICT planning, indicating the relevant subject contexts for developing the ICT outcomes.**

For example, a Year 3 teacher identified that the ICT focus for the coming half-term (five weeks' work) was to be based on Unit 3A of the **QCA ICT Scheme of Work – combining text and graphics**. *The QCA unit described clear objectives for the tasks:*

- *recognise key features of layout;*
- *alter the look of text to create an effect;*
- *amend text and save work;*
- *combine graphics and text;*
- *amend text using the correct key combinations;*
- *combine graphics and text.*

Having identified these key ICT objectives for the five weeks, she then checked over her planning for the other subjects.

Her focus for literacy was to be:

- *reinforcing spelling of high frequency words;*
- *spelling new words by letter strings and analogy;*
- *prefixes;*
- *finding synonyms for high frequency words;*
- *using punctuation when reading;*
- *reinforcing the use of full stop and capital letter for sentences and commas for lists;*
- *identifying verbs in sentences;*
- *identifying direct speech;*
- *poetry – shape poems and emotions;*
- *recognising the difference between fiction and non-fiction;*
- *making use of contents, indexes, headings and page numbers.*

In the other subjects, the children would be covering:

- *numeracy – place value, addition and subtraction;*
- *science – teeth and healthy eating;*
- *geography – our locality;*
- *art – portraits and relationships;*
- *RE/PHSE – relationships – being a good friend;*
- *PE – dance (related to emotions);*
- *music – singing – silly songs.*

As she went through her subject planning she identified a number of places where she could enhance the children's learning through the use of ICT. In addition to her weekly lesson in the ICT suite, she had two classroom computers, one of which she often used for group work.

She then completed her medium-term plan for ICT, showing where and when the objectives she had identified for ICT could be developed (see overleaf).

*This medium-term plan includes only the first three weeks' activities but the teacher continued into the following two weeks by getting the children to write about their locality using the digital photos they had taken as inspiration. The children also completed unfinished limericks and generated their own limericks on screen in their literacy lessons using the word processor and a website (**http://ambleweb.digital-brain.com/ambleweb/ambleweb/ambleweb/year4/limerick.htm**).*

Planning ICT activities to integrate with subject teaching in this way ensures that ICT lessons taught in the ICT suite complement teaching which is going on in the other subjects and that some of the activities which children complete on classroom-based computers in subject lesson time are designed to develop ICT capabilities in a systematic and focused way.

ICT medium-term planning grid

School: Erehwon First School | **Class/Age**: Y3 | **Planning period**: Autumn half-term 1

Key ICT teaching objectives:

By the end of the half term all of the children will be able to:

- **recognise key features of layout;**
- **alter the look of text to create an effect;**
- **amend text and save their work;**
- **combine graphics and text – including clip art and digital photo images;**
- **amend text using the correct key combinations;**
- **evaluate and justify the effect of changing the appearance of text.**

Activity	ICT programme of study	Curriculum context	ICT objectives	Content	Resources (Hardware, software, time)	Classroom organisation	Assessment evidence
1	Exchanging and sharing information – KS2 – 3a	**Literacy – week 1** replacing high frequency words (nice/nasty) with alternatives **Science – week 1** Writing frame - taste experiment **Geography – week 1** Writing frame – My route to school	• **To reinforce basic skills in editing text** • **To check all can use TextEase** • **To use word banks and writing frames** • **To use the spellchecker** • **To save a file to floppy disk**	**Literacy** – completing e-worksheet – word bank to replace high frequency words **Science** – writing frame to write up taste experiment – inserting images **Geography** – writing frame describing their route to school (support group)	2 PCs (classroom-based) TextEase 5 x 20 minutes (literacy) = 20 chn 2 x 30 min (science) = 8 chn 2 x 30 min (geography) = 8 chn Nice/nasty passage Word bank Writing frame (science experiment) Writing frame (route to school)	Pairs working on focused tasks related to subject theme Peer tutors to be available for those who need help (peer tutors to be briefed on Monday)	• **All HF words replaced by words from word bank** • **Writing frames completed well** • **Children not seeking too much help** • **Save a file to floppy disk without assistance**
2	Exchanging and sharing information – KS2 – 3a Reviewing and evaluating KS2 – 4a, c	Literacy – week 1	• **To enhance a piece of text by changing the layout** • **To use font, size, bold, underline, italic** • **To evaluate the effect of changing layout on a piece of text**	Skeleton text based on class book provided with no formatting – children to change font, add headings, add paragraphs and use bold/italics to enhance readability. Plenary to evaluate improvements	15 internet PCs (timetabled 1 hour per week) Interactive whiteboard TextEase Skeleton text	Whole-class introduction Working in twos and threes with support from teaching assistant	• **Use font size, bold, italic, etc.** • **Quality of changes made to skeleton text** • **Justifications made for choices (in lesson and plenary)** • **Able to evaluate own and others' changes**
3	Exchanging and sharing information – KS2 – 3a	**Literacy – week 2** Adding punctuation to text **Science – week 2** Writing frame – teeth **Geography – week 2** Writing frame – Route to school	• **Edit text by adding punctuation** • **Add clip art to a document**	**Literacy** – various e-worksheets with skeleton texts for punctuation to be added – picture inserted from clip art **Science** – writing frame about teeth **Geography** – writing frame – route to school	2 PCs (classroom-based) TextEase 5 x 20 minutes (literacy) = 20 chn 2 x 30 min (science) = 8 chn 2 x 30 min (geography) = 8 chn Differentiated e-worksheets Writing frames	Pairs working on focused tasks related to subject theme Peer tutors to be available for those who need help (peer tutors to be briefed on Monday)	• **Punctuation inserted as required** • **Appropriate images found and inserted**

ICT medium-term planning grid

4 **Exchanging and sharing information – KS2 – 3a** **Reviewing and evaluating KS2 – 4a, c**	**Literacy** – week 2 Sequencing pictures and adding captions to retell a story	• **To use drag and drop editing** • **To enter text from a word bank and from the keyboard** • **To review the content and appearance of their own and each other's work**	Scanned images from class story to be sequenced (drag and drop) and captions added either from word bank (less able) or typed in (more able) or a combination. Plenary to review and evaluate	15 internet PCs TextEase 1-hour ICT lesson Scanned images from story book Word bank E-worksheet of images and text	Whole-class introduction Working in twos and threes with support from teaching assistant	• **Correct sequencing of images** • **Minimum of help required** • **Amount of text entered** • **Extent to which word bank is or is not used**
5 **Exchanging and sharing information – KS2 – 3a**	**Literacy** – week 3 Verbs e-worksheet **Science** – week 3 Writing frame – teeth **Geography** – week 3 Taking digital photos	• **To change text colour and use bold (to highlight verbs)** • **To copy and paste text** • **To create digital images and upload to computer**	**Literacy** – highlighting verbs in extract from story frame (copy and paste) **Science** – teeth writing frame (copy and paste sentences) **Geography** – walk in locality – digital images	2 PCs (classroom-based) TextEase 5 x 20 minutes (literacy) = 20 chn 4 x 15 minutes (science) = 16 chn 2 digital cameras Verb worksheets Writing frames	Pairs working on focused tasks related to subject theme Peer tutors to be available for those who need help (peer tutors to be briefed on Monday)	• **Verbs highlighted appropriately** • **Sentences correctly copied and pasted** • **Digital photos of good quality**
6 **Exchanging and sharing information – KS2 – 3a**	**Art** – week 3 Using paint tools to create portraits **Literacy** – week 3 writing a wanted poster description	• **To describe the function of various paint tools (zoom, shape, spray, brush, pencil, line, fill)** • **To use appropriate paint tools to give themselves a disguise** • **To insert a picture into template document** • **To write a description using cut and paste**	Digital photos taken by teacher and saved on network drive Demonstration by teacher of paint tools Children photo using paint tools Save image as JPEG Insert image into TextEase Wanted poster template Write a description using words from word bank Save TextEase document	15 Internet PCs TextEase 1-hour ICT lesson Scanned images from story book Word bank E-worksheet of images and text	Whole-class introduction Working in twos and threes with support from teaching assistant	• **Good range of different tools and techniques used** • **Image saved and inserted with minimal assistance** • **Words inserted from list using cut and paste**
7 **Exchanging and sharing information – KS2 – 3a** **Reviewing and evaluating KS2 – 4a, c**	**Literacy** – week 4	• **To use font editing tools to present a poem** • **To select and insert digital image and clip art** • **To justify choices of font and layout to convey message**	Brainstorming words and phrases for poem about my friend Teacher makes word bank and places on network drive Children edit document to produce their own poem Insert clip art and digital image of friend	15 internet PCs TextEase 1-hour ICT lesson	Whole-class introduction Working in twos and threes with support from teaching assistant	• **Presentation of poem shows thought about layout** • **Images inserted and presented with minimal help**

MANAGING ASSESSMENT AND RECORD-KEEPING

Many teachers find the assessment of ICT difficult:

> *Despite some improvement, the quality and use of ongoing assessment [in ICT] remain unsatisfactory in over one quarter of schools.*

(OFSTED, 2002a, p. 3)

Because ICT is integrated into the learning and teaching of other subjects it is sometimes difficult to tease out the subject learning from the development of ICT knowledge and skills. As with any aspect of teaching, effective assessment relies on clearly focused planning. If you have a clear awareness of the objectives for a lesson or activity, then the assessment ought to be little more than looking for evidence as to how well the children have achieved those objectives.

As we have seen in the section above, the key to successful ICT teaching lies in having a clearly defined medium-term plan. A suggested approach to assessment is therefore to monitor the children's progress in relation to the learning objectives which have been identified in the medium-term plan and use this information to target teaching and future planning on the needs of the children. The final column of the example medium-term plan shows the sorts of evidence children might demonstrate to show that they have achieved the objectives.

An example of a record-keeping sheet, which logs the children's progress in relation to the above objectives, is shown opposite. This has been created in a word processor by copying and pasting the objectives from the medium-term plan.

MANAGING TIME

The management of time is another important factor in making effective use of ICT resources.

COMPUTER SUITES

Centrally located ICT resources such as computer suites are usually timetabled to ensure that all classes have equal access. However, there will inevitably be times when it is not convenient to make use of time allocated and other occasions when the use of ICT would be highly appropriate outside timetabled slots. Even where ICT suites are rigorously timetabled there is often room for renegotiation between individual teachers. In some schools, the computer suite is not timetabled for morning sessions on the assumption that there is insufficient time in literacy and numeracy lessons for productive ICT usage. Some schools set aside a week-long slot for each class through the year on the basis that this time can be spent in an intensive ICT-based project. It is always worthwhile discussing with colleagues the most effective way such a valuable resource can be deployed, particularly if you are anxious to organise a project which makes more ambitious use of ICT equipment.

Class Y3
ICT Medium-term record – Autumn Term 1

Key
/ = visited
∧ = reinforced
△ = secure

	James Baker	Simon Carter	May Dee	Sarah Elrood	Faye Fennel	Emma Galt	Rodri Hamilton	Gemma Jones	Harry Kirk	Leeroy Lester	Jo Masters	Simone Nuttall	Mariss Openshaw	Darius Plummer	Charlotte Quirk	Denyse Roper	Gray Smith	Toni Turner	Jak Utach	Lemuel Vine	Kristen Walker	Kirsty Young	Jason Zacharius
recognise key features of layout																							
alter the look of text to create an effect																							
enhance a piece of text by changing the layout		/	/	/		/	/	/	△	∧	∧	/		/	△	/	/		/	∧	∧	∧	/
change text colour and use bold (to highlight verbs)																							/
amend text and save their work																							
basic skills in editing text																							
use TextEase																							
save a file to floppy disk																							
combine graphics and text																							
add clip art to a document																							
create digital images and upload to computer																							
describe the function of various paint tools																							
use appropriate paint tools to give themselves a disguise																							
insert a picture into template document																							
select and insert digital image and clip art																							
amend text using the correct key combinations																							
use word banks and writing frames																							
enter text from a word bank and from the keyboard																							
use the spellchecker																							
use font, size, bold, underline, italic																							
edit text by adding punctuation																							
use drag and drop editing																							
copy and paste text																							
evaluate and justify effects																							
evaluate the effect of changing layout on a piece of text																							
review appearance of own and others' work																							
justify choices of font and layout to convey message																							

CLASSROOM-BASED COMPUTERS

For those teachers who have classroom-based computers, the management of access to ICT is more within their control. It might be significant that a study carried out in 2000 (Twining, 2000) indicated that in primary schools classroom computers are used only 50% of the time. Clearly there are times when it is not convenient or appropriate for children to be using a computer, particularly during whole-class teaching sessions. However, as has been shown, the computer can be used as a resource for whole-class teaching which, albeit vicariously, could be contributing to children's knowledge of ICT but certainly conveys the message that the teacher finds ICT to be a useful tool.

The most obvious time for the classroom computer(s) to be used to support English is during the 20 minutes of the literacy hour devoted to independent and group work. In Chapter 4, various computer-based activities were described to complement paper-based work which other children could be completing. Similarly, some of the activities described in Chapter 6 and on the professional development CD ROM for supporting whole-class teaching (DfES, 2001, 2003) could be used for group-based guided writing and guided reading tasks, with a small group of children clustered around the computer screen or interactive whiteboard.

Provided your medium-term planning for ICT has identified the English contexts for developing ICT capabilities, then classroom-based computers can be used at any other convenient time for individuals and pairs to complete ongoing work during sessions which have a more flexible focus (e.g. project time, finishing-off time, reading time, when other work has been finished early, etc.).

Some teachers use a rota system for allocation of the classroom computers. Theoretically, it should be possible for every child to work with a partner for at least an hour each week if two classroom computers are available. However, for this to work, the teacher needs to have a well-organised approach to ensuring that the children have opportunities to complete their other classwork. This can be achieved in a number of ways:

- **ensuring the ICT rota is organised so that the pairs do not miss the same subject sessions each week;**
- **ensuring that every lesson includes a parallel ICT-based activity which relates to the subject and the ICT objectives;**
- **planning weekly tasks on a rolling basis so that children can complete them in any order;**
- **organising project time in which children complete previously started work set out in a weekly to-do list;**
- **accepting that not every child needs to complete every task in every subject (some might be absent anyway);**
- **detailing children to instruct those using the computer(s) about what they have missed;**
- **planning group-based tasks which always include an ICT-based activity for completion by the relevant ICT pair for that session.**

An alternative approach is to encourage children to see the computer as a tool which can be used when it is needed by loading, for example, an electronic dictionary or thesaurus which is available at all times for checking spellings and synonyms. With the introduction of broadband-access to the internet, it is possible for the classroom computer to be connected continuously to a website providing information or online activities relevant to the topic being studied.

Finally, some teachers load the classroom computer each day with a drill and practice program to enable children to practise, for example, their spelling. In turn, each child logs into the program and spends around 15 minutes working through a tailored spelling list. When a child has finished, the computer logs the results (some programs will print out a report) and the child quietly alerts the next on the list to take her turn. This type of activity is only successful if the teacher has created individual word lists for each child based on an analysis of their persistent errors.

MANAGING RESOURCES

ICT resources fall into three categories:

- **hardware – the equipment such as computers, networking, printers, digital cameras, etc.;**
- **software – computer programs;**
- **support materials and consumables – instruction manuals, floppy disks, CD ROMs, printer paper, ink cartridges, etc.**

HARDWARE

As has been mentioned above, the deployment of computers is largely a school-based decision (whether the computers will be centrally pooled in a suite, distributed around classrooms or a combination of both).

When deciding where to position a classroom computer the following might prove useful.

- **If it is to be used for whole-class teaching as well as independent work and group-based activities, it should be positioned conveniently for all purposes, or be mobile.**
- **When being used for independent activities, you might want it positioned to cause the least distraction to others.**
- **The computer should be as close as possible to its power socket and, where relevant, the network point. If extension leads are required, these should not be trailed across thoroughfares.**

You might want to equip the computer with headphones (a splitter plug can be purchased from most computer or electronic suppliers to allow two sets to be plugged into one computer), particularly if you intend using CD ROM packages.

Teachers need also to be aware of basic health and safety considerations when using ICT equipment. More detailed information and guidance is provided on the internet (e.g. **http://safety.ngfl.gov.uk/schools/document.php3?D=d9**) but essentially when organising your ICT equipment you should pay attention to:

- **safe use of electrical equipment;**
- **the positioning of equipment;**
- **child protection issues.**

Safe use of electrical equipment:

- **do not allow children to plug and unplug mains equipment;**
- **keep water well away from any electrical equipment.**

The positioning of equipment:

- **ensure the screen does not reflect bright lights;**
- **use adjustable seating to allow the children to work with their feet on the floor, with the monitor level with their eye-line, and their elbows level with the keyboard;**
- **check the screen is not positioned to distract others.**

Child protection issues:

- **ensure children are not permitted to access the internet without direct supervision from an adult;**
- **ensure children are aware they should not give their names or any other personal details to anyone over the internet;**
- **check children's names are not displayed alongside their pictures on the internet.**

The school should have more detailed policies and procedures for use of ICT equipment, particularly when using the internet and/or when taking digitised images of children. You must make sure you are familiar with these before attempting any ICT work with children, particularly when using the internet.

Another important health and safety consideration is the positioning of data projectors. The intensity of light from these projectors is such that permanent damage to the eye can result from looking into the lens for as little as 5 seconds. As a teacher, you should avoid standing in the beam for prolonged periods, even if you are not looking directly into the lens. Equally importantly, if you are encouraging children to interact with a whiteboard, you should ensure that they look at the screen rather than into the projector lens.

SOFTWARE

Software and files need managing on a computer or a computer network to ensure that children and you as their teacher can find what is needed. Once a computer program has been installed, it will usually be found by accessing the Start menu. Some school-based computers use an educational management program which presents the children with restricted access to the computer's services. With some systems, the installation of new programs can be very cumbersome and time-consuming; it is important you find out how to operate your computer and its software as soon as possible. It is also very important to discover the school's policy on the installation of programs and the downloading of materials from the internet.

Many primary schools are now installing local networks which not only provide all classroom computers with access to the internet, they might also provide teachers with a network drive on to which can be placed files for use by the children. Often children are provided with designated spaces into which they can save their work once they have logged on. Again, it is important to familiarise yourself with these facilities as soon as you join a school to ensure you are able to make maximum and effective use of these resources.

Many teachers, particularly those working with young children, make use of CD ROM-based packages which need to be present in the CD drive to operate. It is important to encourage and develop well-organised routines with the children so they know how to insert and extract the CDs, how to handle them without touching the surface and how and where to store them when not in use. Some schools have invested in CD stacks which enable CDs to be accessed via the school network. Checking what is available and how it can be accessed and installed is another valuable exercise on joining a school.

Chapter 8 outlines sources for software and indicates the types of software which could be considered for use to support the teaching of English.

MANAGING SUPPORT MATERIALS

Most computer programs include on-screen help and information. Some educational programs even include on-screen video sequences demonstrating basic techniques for the children. Inevitably, there will come a time when a program goes wrong or a child asks you to help them do something which you have not done before. Occasionally, you will find yourself in a situation where you simply have forgotten how to do something with a program which you know you have done before. Knowing how to use the on-screen help, or having a copy of the program's manual to hand is an invaluable strategy.

You would not think of starting a lesson without having checked there is paper for the children to write on or pencils available for them to use. Similarly, it is important to ensure that materials which children might need to complete an ICT-based task are prepared beforehand (e.g. paper in the printer, a spare ink cartridge to hand, floppy disks on which to save the children's work, etc.).

COPYRIGHT

Finally, it is very important you are familiar with the laws relating to copyright, particularly if you intend photocopying or scanning published material or making use of web-based text, pictures or other resources on your school's website. Similarly, it is illegal to copy computer programs or CD ROMs without the agreement of the company producing them. It is also illegal to install a program on more than one computer unless a licence has been purchased to permit this. The laws are very strict regarding the use of others' work and prosecutions are not unknown. Ignorance is not an acceptable plea in defence and I doubt a headteacher or board of governors would be sympathetic if your actions resulted in the school facing a heavy fine and adverse publicity.

For more information on the rules relating to copyright and other legal matters (e.g. data protection) refer to **http://safety.ngfl.gov.uk/schools/document.php3?D=d9**

MANAGING PEOPLE

The management of children when making use of ICT equipment in the classroom has been outlined above as this is largely an issue of organising the resources and managing time, but what of managing children in the ICT suite?

MAKING EFFECTIVE USE OF AN ICT SUITE

Effective use of an ICT suite can really only be achieved if it has either a data projector and screen or central control of the children's computers through the teacher's computer. Attempting to teach ICT successfully in a suite without this sort of equipment is a managerial nightmare and can really only be attempted if the teacher has assistance from at least one, but preferably several, adult helpers.

The basic structure of a suite-based ICT lesson is:

- **whole-class introduction/demonstration by the teacher;**
- **explanation of task(s);**
- **children carry out task independently or with a partner – teacher/helpers assist, intervene and guide as required;**
- **mini-plenary, reinforcing what they have already done, demonstrating good examples, demonstrating the next stage, explaining the next task(s);**

and so on.

An alternative approach is to provide the children with prompt sheets or tutorial booklets explaining and illustrating, step by step, what the children need to do. After an initial explanation, the children work through the sheet/booklet at their own pace. This approach is really only successful with older children, however.

Clearly, if other adults such as teaching assistants or parent helpers are used, they need to be well briefed and confident in their use of the ICT equipment. They also need to be given information before the lesson about the ICT and English objectives for the activity to ensure that their assistance and interventions are focused on helping children achieve the desired outcomes. Their assessments of the children's progress after the lesson are also invaluable in deciding whether the children are ready to move on to the next stage or if they need more time consolidating and completing what has been covered in the lesson.

SUBJECT CO-ORDINATORS

The role of the co-ordinator in any school is to check that their subject is being taught successfully and ensure that the resources, information and curriculum are organised and suitably accessible for the teachers and children to accomplish this aim. In some schools, co-ordinators are provided with some non-contact time to work alongside tea-chers to develop and share good practice. In most schools, co-ordinators oversee planning in their subjects and offer suggestions, guidance and advice on activities, resources and background information to enhance and/or co-ordinate the teaching through the school.

ICT co-ordinators often have a more complex role than literacy co-ordinators. They are often called upon to fix temperamental equipment and to advise on the use of ICT across all subject areas, in addition to managing the acquisition and deployment of resources through the school. Literacy co-ordinators tend to have a much tighter brief but have the added responsibility of ensuring children and staff are adequately prepared for SATs preparation and testing.

Some schools also have a separate assessment co-ordinator who has overall responsibil-ity for organising assessment arrangements, record-keeping approaches and the annual parental reporting process.

If you are new to a school it is very important to find out who co-ordinates what and, when planning to integrate ICT into subject teaching, what resources and curriculum support already exists.

In most cases, co-ordinators are only too happy to support teachers who are interested, willing and keen to develop their approaches to teaching within the co-ordinator's subject area.

SUMMARY OF KEY POINTS

- **The key to successful use of ICT in the primary classroom is well-organised medium-term planning.**

- **Managing time, children and resources is central to effective use of ICT.**

- **You should familiarise yourself with health and safety requirements before making use of computers and particularly if you are intending to use the internet.**

- **The laws relating to copyright are very strict and will affect your use of published and web-based materials.**

8 ICT resources and the teaching of English

One of the difficulties when first trying to incorporate ICT into your teaching is finding the right sort of resources to use from the vast range which is available. For example, searching the website of a well known general supplier of educational software for titles associated with English will provide you with a list of 483 programs. Similarly, search for 'English primary teaching resources' using a UK search engine on the internet and you will be presented with 87,700 hits. As with anything, making a judgement about what is good or effective is largely subjective as it will be based on personal knowledge and understanding of both ICT and English, preferred styles of teaching, the equipment you have available, the needs of the children and the topics being studied.

The best advice I was given many years ago in the early days of computers in schools was 'use a small number of resources and use them well'. There is no point in trying to discover every available program or website which might be relevant to the teaching of a particular topic – there simply will not be enough time to use them. Using content-free open-ended software such as a good word processor will be sufficiently adaptable to meet most needs and will be developing the children's ICT capabilities far more effectively than the most attractively presented CD ROM or internet based activities.

This chapter outlines a fairly selective list of what is available to support your teaching and children's learning of English with ICT. It covers the following:

- **hardware resources for English;**
- **software for English;**
- **internet resources.**

No list of resources can ever be exhaustive and so it is worthwhile checking the internet and software providers on a regular basis for new developments.

HARDWARE RESOURCES FOR ENGLISH

In previous chapters some hardware has been mentioned, such as plasma screens, data projectors and interactive whiteboards. Although these resources are not essential, they do make the teaching of some aspects of English, particularly whole-class teaching, a lot easier.

Interactive whiteboards are very expensive and are not essential for children to interact with what is on the screen. As has been mentioned in Chapter 7, a remote keyboard and mouse can be passed around the classroom for children to use with a projected image of the screen.

For very young children, keyboards can be purchased which show the letters in lower case – very useful when children are in the early stages of letter recognition. Concept keyboards provide the children with a large flat area either A3 or A4 sized onto which can be placed an overlay. The children press on the pictures or words printed on the overlay to make things happen on the computer screen. Concept keyboards were very popular in schools before the advent of computers with a mouse and a windows environment but are still very useful for very young children or those who find using a conventional keyboard difficult.

A useful device for helping children practise handwriting, among other activities, is a graphics pad. Usually around the size of an A5 sheet of paper, these sit beside the normal keyboard and control the movement of the pointer on screen by drawing with a stylus on the pad. They are designed for use by graphic artists who need a fine level of control, but are equally suitable for those practising control of a pencil by tracing over letters on screen.

Other hardware resources which could be considered are those which provide access and support for children with sensory or motor difficulties. A wide range of input devices is available to augment or replace the keyboard and/or mouse. For example, a roller ball controls the movement of the pointer on screen by rolling a ball fixed in a cradle. Some programs can be used with special switches which can be operated by children with restricted movement.

Pocket or handheld computers with keyboards enable children to enter text which can later be edited using a full-sized word processor (see Griffiths, 2003). Their size means they can be carried around easily, on an educational visit for example, and their price means that several could be purchased for the cost of a single desktop or laptop computer. They can also be taken home by children to complete work and provide valuable hands-on experience with word processing and editing.

Electronic spellcheckers can prove more useful than dictionaries in helping children spell unknown words, particularly if they include phonic equivalents. For example, entering 'ekwivalant' will produce suggestions of 'equivalent' or 'equivalents'. Some also include word games such as hangman and can produce anagrams and help solve crossword clues.

SOFTWARE

Generally, software can be sorted into two overall categories:

- **content-free or open-ended software;**
- **content-specific software.**

CONTENT-FREE SOFTWARE

Content-free software is usually a tool which can be used for a multitude of different purposes. The content-free software which is appropriate for English teaching includes the following types of program:

- *Educational draw packages.* **A draw package differs from a paint package in that every shape which is drawn on screen becomes a separate object which can be dragged and dropped, resized and easily copied and pasted. Draw packages are** especially useful for young children as they can drag and drop objects to construct their own pictures, or to match words to pictures, or drag objects comprising letters, graphemes, words, phrases and sentences.

- *Educational art packages.* Educational art packages offer a range of tools which enable children to create their own pictures, either by starting with a blank screen or by editing existing pictures. Uses of paint packages for English teaching include adding captions to pictures and creating illustrations and diagrams for illustrated texts.

- *Educational word processors.* Educational word processors include additional features to enhance children's learning such as word banks, text-to-speech and configurable toolbars and/or levels. Some include additional spellchecking options (e.g. recording common errors), drawing tools (including drag and drop) and clip art libraries appropriate for the primary classroom.

- *Desktop publishing packages.* Many word processors now include many of the tools which formerly were found only on desktop publishing packages (e.g. text frames, images frames, page preview). Desktop publishing (DTP) packages include a wide range of templates for documents such as flyers, posters, brochures, adverts, newsletters and so on which benefit from layouts designed by professional graphic artists.

- *Presentation software.* Originally designed for use in commercial settings, presentation software allows the user to create a series of 'slides' linked together to communicate information in the form of text and images, often using animation and sound effects to enhance interest. Presentation tools are useful for teachers, particularly those with interactive whiteboards, but are valuable for helping children to identify and communicate key facts about a topic.

- *Multimedia authoring software.* Whereas presentation software is designed primarily for creating slide shows which present a series of screens in sequence, multimedia presentations assume that the user will work their own way through the screen by clicking on buttons and hyperlinks. CD ROM encyclopaedias and most websites are examples of multimedia presentations; readers find their own way through the information by clicking on links and accessing the information through text, images, animations, and sound and video clips. For children, communicating their knowledge through multimedia is not only motivating but enables them to create information sources which mirror those which form part of their everyday experience. Commercial multimedia authoring tools are used by software companies to produce CD ROM packages and websites and are consequently expensive, but multimedia authoring packages appropriate for schools are well established.

- *Multimedia story-making software.* A refinement on general multimedia authoring packages but highly appropriate for supporting literacy learning, story-making packages tend to include clip art, animations, sounds and tools specific to the writing of linear and/or branching stories.

- *Web page authoring software.* The internet provides children with an immediate worldwide audience for their work in multimedia format. Creating a web page is little more difficult than word processing – in fact, most word processors and desktop publishing packages include an option to save a document as a web page.

However, when creating web pages with software other than web authoring programs the layout of the web page does not always resemble the way it appeared when it was created.

- *Databases.* Databases come in a range of different formats, but the most familiar is probably that which resembles a card index system. Each screen represents a record of information about a given topic (e.g. each screen shows information about a particular child in a class). The speed with which a large amount of information can be searched and sorted with a computer means that databases are used extensively for handling data. Processing information so that it can be presented in a compact yet meaningful format is an important literacy skill, as is searching for and locating the information which is required to answer an enquiry. Commercial databases tend to be complex and overly complicated but there is a wide range of educational databases to suit all age ranges.

- *Mind-mapping, flowcharting and brainstorming software.* A recent upsurge in interest in the development of thinking skills in the primary school has resulted in the development of software tools which support concept mapping and flow-charting. Representing knowledge and understanding by means of these tools enables the teacher to gain an appreciation of the children's current knowledge and understanding of a topic and helps the children frame their thoughts by formulating relationships between seemingly disparate ideas.

There is more software which fits into the category of 'content-free' such as spread-sheets, LOGO programming tools, graphing programs and photo-editing packages. While some of these may have an indirect application for English teaching and learning, they are not specifically associated with literacy.

CONTENT-SPECIFIC SOFTWARE

Content-specific software, as the name suggests, covers programs which are designed for a specific purpose. The content of the software has been determined by the software designers and developers, and the form of presentation makes assumptions about the way children learn. Content-specific software should be chosen carefully, particularly if it does not include features enabling the teacher to extend the content or configure the way the information or tasks are presented.

Content-specific software includes the following, relevant to the teaching of English:

- *CD ROM encyclopaedias and information sources.* CD ROM encyclopaedias were originally developed as electronic versions of well-known paper-based encyclo-paedias, with the addition of a few sound clips and video sequences. In more recent times they have become highly sophisticated information sources which make effective use of interactive features enabling readers to browse their way through information following their interests and needs. Children need to develop skills, not only in searching and browsing for information (two quite different skills), but also in recognising when a CD ROM encyclopaedia might be the most appropriate source of information. In addition, some CD ROM sources allow users to copy and paste information and images into their own documents. Clearly, children need to know how to rework this information to answer their own enquiries.

- *Drill and practice software.* The most common drill and practice program found in classrooms is for practising spelling. Drill and practice programs tend to be highly focused on reinforcing learning in a specific area of the curriculum. Those which are most useful include options for the teacher to tailor the content and the presentation for specific groups or individuals. Others provide information on individual children's progress which teachers can access to inform their assessment of the children and subsequent teaching.

- *Integrated learning systems.* ILSs are very expensive sophisticated versions of drill and practice software. Each child is provided with a series of activities 'tailored' to their needs based on their responses to previous questions. As was seen in Chapter I, research findings are equivocal over the efficacy of this approach to learning and teaching.

- *Problem-solving software.* Simulations and adventure programs fall into this category, as does any program which encourages the children to think, make decisions and see the results of their decisions. Some online puzzles provide considerable challenge and knowledge of the way the English language works, such as the cryptogram puzzle on the www.thesaurus.com website.

- *Software tools.* These are software tools which add functionality to your computer. For example, a spellchecker tool can be added which will check spelling in any program. Other programs provide the children with a specially prepared windows environment which prevents them from tampering with the settings and ensures their work is saved in a designated folder. Other tools intercept unsuitable websites and prevent them from being shown or detect when a virus is about to infect a computer. Tools such as these can ensure that a school computer runs more reliably and appropriately for children's use.

Information about software suitable for use in primary English teaching can be found at any of the following sources:

- the TEEM website;
- the BECTa CD ROM evaluation database;
- BETT.

TEEM (TEACHERS EVALUATING EDUCATIONAL MULTIMEDIA) (www.teem.org.uk)

This website was established to provide independent advice for teachers on the educational value of software. Teachers are provided with programs for use in their classrooms on condition they write a report and a case study on its use. As a consequence, the information on the website is provided by real teachers working in real classrooms with real children. Before considering purchasing or using educational software it is well worth checking the TEEM website for an evaluation.

THE BECTa EDUCATIONAL SOFTWARE DATABASE (BESDA)

BESDA enables you to search for programs that fit particular criteria (e.g. age group, subject, key word, etc.) and provides you with a brief outline of the content plus a link to the software supplier's website.

BETT, SETT AND THE EDUCATION SHOW

The BETT (British Educational Technology and Training) Show is held every year in London at the beginning of January. Practically every supplier of educational technology is represented and it provides an opportunity for teachers to see, try and discuss educational software and equipment first hand. In addition, there are seminars and presentations by leading figures in the world of educational technology, including government ministers who sometimes launch the latest ICT initiative at the show. BETT probably offers the greatest opportunity for those interested in ICT to find out what is available and how it works. The Scottish equivalent (SETT) is usually held in September and the Education Show is usually held at the NEC (Birmingham) in March.

INTERNET RESOURCES

The rapid growth of the internet and the vast array of information it provides is a mixed blessing and also provides learners with new challenges in locating, evaluating and manipulating the information which is provided. Not only do children need to know how to find relevant information, they need to know how to judge its relevance, reliability and accuracy. It is also very important that children are made aware of the dangers associated with use of the internet and know how to protect their identities and safeguard their computers.

Websites also provide teachers and learners with interactive games and activities, many of which are designed to support learning. Some activities are very well implemented with a sound basis in educational practices. Others are of dubious educational merit. As a teacher, you need to thoroughly examine the educational value of web-based activities to ensure they address the learning objectives you have identified for a topic.

Websites appropriate for supporting the teaching of English are wide and varied and fall into the following categories:

- **government and national organisations;**
- **websites for primary teachers;**
- **websites for children;**
- **shareware libraries;**
- **educational software suppliers.**

What follows is a representative selection of what is available. A few hours spent searching the internet will yield many more.

GOVERNMENT AND NATIONAL ORGANISATIONS

The websites for government departments and national organisations offer up-to-date information and documents relating to current trends in teaching and learning.

Government sites:

Department for Education and Skills – **www.dfes.gov.uk/index.htm**
UK Teachernet (lesson plans etc.) – **www.teachernet.gov.uk**
DFES Standards site – **www.standards.dfee.gov.uk**

Literacy Strategy – **www.standards.dfee.gov.uk/literacy**
National Curriculum online – **www.nc.uk.net/index.html**
Basic Skills Agency (the national development organisation for literacy and numeracy)
   – **www.basic-skills.co.uk/**
British Education and Communications Technology Agency – **www.becta.org.uk**
National Grid for Learning (NGfL) – **www.ngfl.gov.uk/**
Teachers' Resource Exchange – **http://tre.ngfl.gov.uk/**
Superhighway Safety website – **http://safety.ngfl.gov.uk/**
Virtual Teachers' Centre (VTC) – **www.vtc.ngfl.gov.uk**
VTC literacy resources – **http://vtc.ngfl.gov.uk/resource/literacy**

National organisations related to teaching English:

Child Literacy Centre – **www.childliteracy.com/index.html**
National Literacy Trust – **www.literacytrust.org.uk/**
National Centre for Language and Literacy – **www.ncll.org.uk/**
National Literacy Association – **www.nla.org.uk/**
UK Reading Association (UKRA) – **www.ukra.org/**
Book Trust – **www.booktrust.org.uk/**
Poetry Society – **www.poetrysociety.org.uk/**
English Association – **www.le.ac.uk/engassoc/**
Reading is Fundamental (RIF) – **www.poetrysociety.org.uk/**
National Association for the Teaching of English (NATE) – **www.nate.org.uk/**
Centre for Language in Primary Education – **www.clpe.co.uk/**

WEBSITES FOR TEACHERS

BECTa Educational software database – **http://besd.becta.org.uk/**
Guide to grammar and writing – **http://webster.commnet.edu/grammar/index.htm**
Literacy Matters – **www.literacymatters.com/**
Literacy Time website – **http://curriculum.becta.org.uk/literacy/index.html**
MAPE – Micros and Primary Education – **www.mape.org.uk/**
Online Writing Lab – **http://owl.english.purdue.edu/handouts/grammar/index.html**
Sites for teachers – **www.sitesforteachers.com/index.html**
Teachers and Writers online – **www.twc.org/**
Teachers Evaluating Educational Multimedia – **www.teem.org.uk/**
The Blue Book of Grammar and Punctuation – online resources –
   www.grammarbook.com/default.htm
Wordpool – information about helping children to become readers –
   www.wordpool.co.uk/
Topmarks for teachers – **www.topmarks.co.uk**
School Express – **www.freeworksheets.com/**
Schoolzone – **www.justforteachers.co.uk/**
English Resources – **www.englishresources.co.uk/**
Click Teaching – **www.clickteaching.com/**
Teaching Ideas for Primary Teachers – **www.teachingideas.co.uk/**
Skills Factory – **www.skillsfactory.com/index.html**

Under Fives Early Years Education – **www.underfives.co.uk/**
Primary Resources – **www.primaryresources.co.uk/**
Create your own school website for free – **www.schools.ik.com**
BT's education website (includes access to free drama workshops) –
　　www.btplc.com/ict/
Reading Matters – **www.readingmatters.co.uk**
Get Netwise – guidance for parents and children on safe internet use –
　　www.getnetwise.org/
Children's handwriting fonts – **http://cgm.cs.mcgill.ca/-luc/kids.html**
Achuka – information about children's books and reading –
　　www.achuka.co.uk/index2.php
Barry's clip art server – free clip art – **www.barrysclipart.com/index.php**

WEBSITES FOR CHILDREN

These range from websites featuring online games practising aspects of literacy, to online stories and poetry, and information about books and authors.

Online stories and poems:

Giggle poetry – poetry fun for KS2 – **www.meadowbrookpress.com/Poetry**
Grimm fairy tales – online talking books – **www.grimmfairytales.com/en/**
　　main
Hans Andersen's Fairy Tales told online – **www.andersenfairytales.com/en/**
　　main
Kidpub – online publishing – **www.kidpub.org/kidpub/**
MAPE online big books – **www.mape.org.uk/kids/bigbooks/index.htm**
Ogden Nash's poetry online – **www.westegg.com/nash/**
Poetry for kids by Kenn Nesbitt – **www.nesbitt.com/poetry/**
Poetry online – **www.poetryonline.com/**
Sebastian Swan's literacy resources (Big Book activities) – **www.naturegrid.**
　　org.uk/infant/literacy.html
Stories from the Web – **www.storiesfromtheweb.org/sfwhomepage.htm**
Story starters – **www.sutton.lincs.sch.uk/pages/zone/story/start.html**
The Mother Goose Page – **www.personal.umich.edu/-pfa/dreamhouse/**
　　nursery/rhymes.html
The Never Ending Tale – **www.coder.com/creations/tale/**
Vocabulary resources – **http://syndicate.com/**
Wacky Web Tales – **www.eduplace.com/tales/**

Online games and puzzles:

Ambleside School's web-based resources for literacy – **http://ambleweb.**
　　digitalbrain. com/ambleweb/ambleweb/ambleweb/literacy.htm
Anagram solver – **www.wordsmith.org/anagram/index.html**
BBC Schools home page – **www.bbc.co.uk/schools/**
Education 4 kids – **www.edu4kids.com/**
Email Santa – **www.claus.com/**
Fake-out – **www.eduplace.com/fakeout**
Fun school – online games – **www.funschool.com/index.html**

Fun with Spot – online activities to accompany the Spot the Dog books –
www.funwithspot.com/

Funbrain.com – **www.funbrain.com/kidscenter.html**

Grammar Gorillas – **www.funbrain.com/grammar/index.html**

Gridclub – **www.gridclub.com/**

Puzzle Maker (from the Discovery Channel) – **www.puzzlemaker.com/**

Santa's Secret Village – **www.northpole.com/Village.html**

Seussville – online games related to Dr Seuss books – **www.seussville.com/
seussville/**

The BigBus – **www.thebigbus.com/**

Information about books and authors:

Kids Bookshelf – **www.kidsbookshelf.com**

Lynch multimedia – online Shakespeare – **www.lynchmultimedia.com/
shakespeare.html**

Mrs Mad's Bookerama – **www.mrsmad.com/**

Puffin books homepage – information, games and puzzles – **www.puffin.co.uk/**

The Book Review site – **http://faldo.atmos.uiuc.edu/bookreview/**

The children's literature web guide – **www.acs.ucalgary.ca/-dkbrown/
index.html**

The Writesite journalism role playing – **www.writesite.org/**

Young Writer – **www.mystworld.com/youngwriter/index.html**

SHAREWARE LIBRARIES

Shareware is primarily software which has been developed by individuals to meet a need which they have identified. It is distributed over the internet and can be downloaded from shareware websites which list thousands of programs covering all manner of topics. Most shareware works on the principle of 'try before you buy', which means a program can be downloaded and installed on your computer; if you decide you want to keep it, you pay a fee to the developer to become a registered user. Before registration the software might have only a limited range of features or might cease to operate after a 30-day period. Shareware ranges in quality and reliability so it is advisable to read any reviews of a program before downloading it. Shareware websites check all downloads for viruses and it is rare that viruses are distributed in this way. However, it is advisable to have an up-to-date antivirus program installed on your computer before downloading anything from the internet.

CNET Download.com (for kids) – **http://download.com/3150-2102-0.
html?tag=dir**

Link-up parents selected shareware – **www.linkup-parents.com/shareware.
htm**

Pass the shareware – **www.passtheshareware.com**

Shareware.com – **www.shareware.com**

Simply the Best shareware (for kids) – **simplythebest.net/shareware/
educational/kids.stuff.html**

Tucows shareware for kids – **tukids.tucows.com**

EDUCATIONAL SOFTWARE SUPPLIERS

It is always worth visiting the websites of educational software developers or suppliers. In addition to detailed information (and sometimes reviews) of their programs, many educational software companies provide free downloadable versions of their software for teachers to try before purchasing. Some companies will allow you to order their software for an evaluation period of up to 28 days, enabling you to use it in your classroom with your children before deciding whether to buy.

The following represents only a sample of those which are available. Those listed are included because they have been specifically mentioned in previous chapters and/or because they include downloadable resources:

4mation – **www.4mation.co.uk**
Crick Software – **www.cricksoft.com/**
Dial Solutions – **www.dialsolutions.com**
Espresso – **www.espresso.co.uk/**
Granada Learning – **www.granada-learning.com/**
GSP – **www.gsp.cc/**
RM plc – **www.rm.com/**
Sherston Software – **www.sherston.co.uk/**
SoftEase – **www.textease.com**
SPA – **www.spasoft.co.uk**
Tag Learning – **www.taglearning.com/**
Topologika – **www.topologika.co.uk**

The following are general educational software suppliers whose websites list a range of programs from various software companies:

REM – **www.r-e-m.co.uk/**
AVP Software – **www.avp.co.uk/**
ESPA – **www.besanet.org.uk/**

FURTHER READING

BACKGROUND INFORMATION ABOUT ENGLISH

Medwell, J., Moore, G., Wray, D. and Griffiths, V. (2001) *Primary English: Knowledge and Understanding.* Exeter: Learning Matters.
Medwell, J., Wray, D., Minns, H., Griffiths, V. and Coates, E. (2001) *Primary English: Teaching Theory and Practice.* Exeter, Learning Matters.

LITERACY AND ICT

Gamble, N. and Easingwood, N. (2000) *ICT and Literacy: Information and Communications Technology, Media, Reading and Writing.* London and New York: Continuum.
Monteith, M. (ed.) (2002) *Teaching Primary Literacy with ICT.* Buckingham: Open University Press.
Singleton, C. (ed.) (1994) *Computers and Dyslexia: Educational Applications of New Technology.* University of Hull, Dyslexia Computer Resource Centre.

Wegerif, R. and Scrimshaw, P. (eds) (1997) *Computers and Talk in the Primary Classroom*. Clevedon: Multilingual Matters.

BOOKS WITH USEFUL CHAPTERS ON ICT AND LITERACY

Basford, J. and Poulter, T. (2003) *Using ICT in Foundation Stage Teaching*. Exeter: Learning Matters.

Cook, D. and Finlayson, H. (1999) *Interactive Children, Communicative Teaching: ICT and Classroom Teaching*. Buckingham: Open University Press.

Loveless, A. and Dore, B. (2002) *ICT in the Primary School*. Buckingham: Open University Press.

McFarlane, A. (ed.) (1997) *Information Technology and Authentic Learning: Realising the Potential of Computers in the Primary Classroom*, London: Routledge.

Sharp, J., Potter, J., Allen, J. and Loveless, A. (2002) *Primary ICT: Knowledge, Understanding and Practice*. Exeter: Learning Matters.

Siraj-Blatchford, J. and Whitebread, D. (2003) *Supporting Information and Communications Technology in the Early Years*. Maidenhead: Open University Press.

References

Abbott, C. (2001) *ICT: Changing Education*. London: RoutledgeFalmer.

BECTa (1998) *The UK ILS Evaluations: Final Report*. Coventry: BECTa.

Bennett, R. and Pearson, H. (2002) ICT and reading: what can software do?, in M. Monteith (ed.) *Teaching Primary Literacy with ICT*. Buckingham: Open University.

Bowell, B., France, S. and Redfern, S. (1994) *Portable Computers in Action*. Coventry: National Centre for Educational Technology.

Dawes, L. and Wegerif, L. (1998) *Encouraging Exploratory Talk: Practical Suggestions*. Newman College, MAPE focus on literacy, Autumn 1998. Available online at **www.mape.org.uk/curriculum/english/exploratory.htm** (accessed March 2004).

Day, J. (1993) *A Software Guide for Specific Learning Difficulties*. Coventry: National Centre for Educational Technology (NCET).

DfEE (1997) *Connecting the Learning Society*. London: DfEE.

DfEE (1998) *The National Literacy Strategy: Framework for Teaching*. London: DfEE.

DfEE/QCA (1999) *The National Curriculum: Handbook for Primary Teachers*. London: DfEE.

DfES (2000) *Phonics – Progression in Phonics for Whole Class Teaching*. London: DfES.

DfES (2001) *ICT in the Literacy Hour: Whole Class Teaching*. London: DfES.

DfES (2002) *Transforming the Way We Learn: A Vision for the Future of ICT in Schools*. London: DfES.

DfES (2003) *ICT in the Literacy Hour: Independent Work and Guided Reading*. London: DfES.

DfES/BECTa (2001) *Evaluation of Computers for Teachers: Phase 1*. London: DfES/BECTa.

DfES/QCA (2003) *A Scheme of Work for Key Stages 1 and 2: Information and Communication Technology: A Teachers' Guide*. London: DfES/QCA.

Dodds, D. (1985) Driller skillers, *Sinclair User*, February. Available online at **www.sincuser.f9.co.uk/035/opinion.htm** (accessed July 2003).

Donaldson, J. (2001) *Room on the Broom*. London: Macmillan.

Easingwood, N. (2000) Electronic communication in the twenty-first century, in N. Gamble and N. Easingwood (eds) *ICT and Literacy: Information and Communications Technology, Media, Reading and Writing*. London: Continuum.

Ellis, V. (2001) Analogue clock/digital display: continuity and change in debates about literacy, technology and English, in A. Loveless and V. Ellis (eds) *ICT, Pedagogy and the Curriculum: Subject to Change*. London: RoutledgeFalmer.

Ferrigan, C. (2001) *Passing the ICT Skills Test*. Exeter: Learning Matters.

Fischer Trust (2002) *High Impact ICT Resources: Primary*. Cowbridge: Fischer Family Trust.

Griffiths, C. (2003) Handheld portable computers. Available online at **www.nla.org.uk.CharlieArticle.htm** (accessed November 2003).

Harrison, C. et al. (2003) *ImpaCT2: The Impact of Information and Communication Technologies on Pupil Learning and Attainment: Full Report*. Coventry: BECTa.

Hunter, P. (1989) The writing process and word-processing. *MicroScope Special*, Summer, Birmingham: Newman College/MAPE.

Kennewell, S., Parkinson, J. and Tanner, H. (2000) *Developing the ICT Capable School*. London: RoutledgeFalmer.

Lancy, D. and Hayes, B. (1988) Interactive fiction and the reluctant reader. *English Journal*, 77(7): 42–6.

Lewin, C. (1996) *Improving Talking Book Software Sesign: Emulating the Supportive Tutor*. CITE Report No. 222. Milton Keynes: Open University.

Lewin, C. (2000) Exploring the effects of talking book software in UK primary classrooms. *Journal of Research in Reading*, 23(2): 149–57.

Loveless, A., DeVoogd, G. L. and Bohlin, R. M. (2001) Something old, something new...: Is pedagogy affected by ICT?, in A. Loveless and V. Ellis (eds) *ICT, Pedagogy and the Curriculum*. London: RoutledgeFalmer.

McFarlane, A. (1997) Thinking about writing, in A. McFarlane (ed.) *Information Technology and Authentic Learning*. London: RoutledgeRoss.

McGarry, K. (1992) Definitions and meanings of literacy, in K. Barker and R. Lonsdale (eds) *Skills for Life? The Meaning and Value of Literacy*. London: Taylor Graham.

Medwell, J. (1995) Talking books for teaching reading, *Microscope*, no. 46.

Medwell, J. (1998) The talking books project: some further insights into the use of talking books to develop reading. *Reading*, April: 3–8.

Meek, M. (1991) *On Being Literate*. London: Bodley Head.

Miles, M. (1994) The Somerset talking computer project', in C. Singleton (ed.) *Computers and Dyslexia: Educational Applications of New Technology*. University of Hull, Dyslexia Computer Resource Centre.

Mills, G. and Walker, H. (2002) Discrete charmers and good mixers: is ICT best taught as a subject or with other subjects? *TES Teacher*, May: 30–31.

Millwood, R. (2000) A new relationship with media, in N. Gamble and N. Easingwood (eds) *ICT and Literacy: Information and Communications Technology, Media, Reading and Writing*. London: Continuum.

Monteith, M. (ed.) *Teaching Primary Literacy with ICT*. Buckingham: Open University Press.

Moseley, D. and Hartas, C. (1993). Say that again, please: a scheme to boost reading skills using a computer with digitised speech. *Support for Learning*, 8(1): 16–21.

Moseley, D. and Higgins, S. (1999) *Ways Forward with ICT: Effective Pedagogy using Information and Communications Technology for Literacy and Numeracy in Primary Schools*. Newcastle: University of Newcastle.

OFSTED (2001) *Primary Subject Reports: Information and Communication Technology 2000/01*. London: OFSTED.

OFSTED (2002a) *Information and Communication Technology in Primary Schools: Ofsted Subject Reports Series 2001/02*. London: OFSTED.

OFSTED (2002b) *The National Literacy Strategy: The First Four Years 1998–2002*. London, OFSTED.

OFSTED (2002c) *ICT in Schools: Effect of Government Initiatives: Implementation in Primary Schools and Effect on Literacy*. London: OFSTED.

Oldfather, P., West, J., White, J. and Wilmarth, J. (1999) *Learning Through Children's Eyes: Social Constructivism and the Desire to Learn*. Washington, DC: American Psychological Association.

Papert, S. (1980) *Mindstorms: Children, Computers and Powerful Ideas*. Brighton: Harvester Press.

Papert, S. (1993) *The Children's Machine: Rethinking School in the Age of the Computer*. New York: Basic Books.

Peters, M. and Cripps, C. (1990) *Catchwords: Ideas for Teaching Spelling*. London: Harcourt, Brace Jovanovich.

Sheingold, K., Hawkins, J. and Carr, C. (1984) I'm the thinkist, you're the typist: the interaction of technology and the social life of classrooms. *Journal of Social Issues*, 40(3): 49–61.

Taylor, C. (1996) Teaching reading with talking story books. *Computer Education*, 84: 24–6.

Twining, P. (2000) *The Computer Practice Framework: A Tool to Help Identify the Impact on Educational Practice of Investments in Information and Communication Technology*. ALT-C 2000, Manchester.

Underwood, J. D. (2000) Comparison of two types of computer support for reading development. *Journal of Research in Reading* 23(2): 136–48.

Underwood, J. D. M. and Underwood, G. (1990) *Computers and Learning: Helping Children Acquire Thinking Skills*. Oxford: Blackwell.

Watson, D. (ed.) (1993) *The Impact Report: An Evaluation of the Impact of Information Technology on Children's Achievements in Primary and Secondary Schools*. London: King's College, Centre for Educational Studies.

Wegerif, R. and Dawes, L. (1988) Encouraging exploratory talk around computers, in M. Monteith (ed.) *IT for Learning Enhancement*. Exeter: Intellect Books.

Wegerif, R. and Dawes, L. (2002) Talking solutions: the role of oracy in the effective use of ICT, in M. Monteith (ed.) *Teaching Primary Literacy with ICT*. Buckingham: Open University.

Wegerif, R., Mercer, N. and Dawes, L. (1998) Integrating pedagogy and software design to support discussion in the primary curriculum. *Journal of Computer Assisted Learning*, 14: 199–211.

Wegerif, R. and Scrimshaw, P. (eds) (1997) *Computers and Talk in the Primary Classroom*. Clevedon: Multilingual Matters.

Wishart, J. M. (1997) Initial teacher training students' attitudes to use of IT and individual locus of control. *Journal of Computer Assisted Learning*, 6(3): 271–84.

Wood, T. (1984) Great expectations. *Sinclair User*, June 1984. available online at **www.sincuser.f9.co.uk/027/eductn.htm** (accessed July 2003).

Wragg, E. C., Wragg, C. M., Haynes, G. S. and Chamberlin, R. P. (1998) *Improving Literacy in the Primary School*. London: Routledge.

Index